Rafa Brites

I0529531

IMPOST-HER SYNDROME

Why We Never Feel Good Enough?

WeBook Publishing - English Edition

This work is based on the author's experience dealing with imposter syndrome. The opinions and methods described within this book are the author's personal findings. You may discover there are other methods and materials to accomplish the same end result. For information, please email info@webookpublishing.com

Copyright © 2025 Rafa Brites

Copyright © 2025 WeBook Publishing

First English Edition

Paperback

ISBN: 978-1-966892-13-7

LCCN: 2025901107

Written by Rafa Brites

Translator: Nathalia Coppa

Editor: Ana Silvani

Copy Editor: Maria Acero

Cover Design: WeBook Publishing

Interior Formatting: Deborah Liss

Manufactured in the United States of America

Note: Much care and technique were employed in editing this book. However, there can be no assurance that it will be free of minor typing errors, printing issues, or even conceptual ambivalence. In any such case, we ask that the issue be notified to our customer service at the e-mail address: info@webookpublishing.com. Thank you!

I dedicate this book to all the women who have ever doubted themselves.

ACKNOWLEDGEMENTS

Thank you to all the women who have deeply inspired me: my grandmothers, aunts, cousins, mother-in-law, godmother, friends, and co-workers. To my niece Miranda, my sisters Gabi and Lú, and Maria do Horto, my beloved mother, I offer you all my love and gratitude.

Of course, thank you to my father, Potiguara, my partner in this journey, Felipe, and the biggest gift life gave me: my children. You make me shine.

CONTENTS

HEY!

It's my pleasure to welcome you here.
Make yourself comfortable on your couch, a chair, the bus seat, or wherever you are. In case your young children are calling you, find some refuge in the bathroom so we can chat a bit about our lives.
I believe we have something very important in common.
You might be on the precipice of finding out:

What is blocking your dreams?
What has held you back from conquering (or enjoying) what you have fought so hard to achieve?
What makes you think that any other person in the world is more qualified?
What made you lose your shine?

Yes, you are going to uncover all of this here as we roam the words and paths I took to evolve in the face of so much insecurity.
Oh, and you can't even imagine how happy I am to gather everything I learned and, finally, write a BOOK. Woohoo!

Calm down.
Did I say "book"?
Wait…
A book I WROTE?!
Why would someone read a book/wrote?

BLANK

That's how the pages of the books I dreamed of writing stayed for years. After all, who am I to publish a book?

I don't have a life story like John Lennon's, a fight like Malala's, nor the knowledge of Stephen Hawkin. I'm not ahead of my time like Simone de Beauvoir.

If only I had majored in Language Arts at HARVARD. Such thoughts had me face questions like: Why even write the book? For whom? And why would someone like you, the reader, with so many options, choose to read Rafa Brites' book?

So why write it?

For whom?

Facing these questions, I had to take action.

> I took a deep breath and thought:
> Yes, you are unique, singular.
> Everyone has something to say.
> Let's write!
> #expectations

> I went to the kitchen, opened the fridge and grabbed a snack. I got my phone and wasted an hour scrolling up and down. Then, I started looking for something that had to be done with urgency: tide up my socks drawer by color and size. And just like that another day went by swallowed by procrastination.
> #reality

I have always loved writing. Whether it was school tests or college entrance exams, my favorite moment was always when it came time to write. Through my writing, I gained most of my social media followers. I became a columnist for a printed magazine. How fancy.

But wait...

A book?

Not a good idea, right, Rafa?

Have you been drinking?

Yes, a little, but that's not important at the moment. Moving on...

As time went on, I noticed that whenever I sat down to write it was like I was trying to trick someone. It felt as if my knowledge was never enough to fill up an entire book. As if, at any moment, while leafing through my book, the reader would discover that I was a fake.

Books are eternal. With fake news running rampant, we couldn't have a *fake book*, can we?

MY INTELLECTUAL CAPACITY

One of my biggest insecurities as an imposter is feeling like I should write in a more elaborate way. Something that would impress the people that impress me, you know? That's why I decided to solve that problem right away. I will present all of my potential in the form of language that I will not be taking advantage of in this book.

According to Nietzsche, we, human beings, coming from fruitful maternal wombs in our insignificant and fleeting existence, inexorably seek meaning in the subjectivity of others despite the dense elements essential to the human psyche.

However, we live unsustainably in pursuit of success within daily tasks, influenced by the rapid march of our ephemeral subsistence.

This is attested by the perspicuous eloquence of Greek eruditeness perpendicularly influenced by the Frankfurt School.

I conjecture that you, venerable reader, did not count on my cunning of writing in such a complicated way.

With simple words, I abstain from any blame and objections that may be attributed to me for not offering you a book with a very elaborate vocabulary.

Grateful,
Rafaella

THE SECRET SOCIETY

THE IMPOSTER THAT LIVES IN ME

As the years went by, I became more bothered with the eternal feeling that nothing I ever did was enough for me to believe in myself. I thought my ideas and projects weren't worth the investment. It irritated me to the point that I decided to dig deeper, comb through the real reasons that caused so much insecurity. I had come from such an incredible family that always supported me, so this didn't make any sense.

So, I started to pay attention to moments in my life where I not only felt like an Imposter but also felt stuck and paralyzed by fear.

ATTENTION:
Get a bucket of popcorn,
and if you have a pet, keep them close.
It might be good to
have something cute to snuggle with.

The worst moment of all happened in 2006 when I was 20 years old. I believe it's the principal and best personal example I have of how the feeling of insufficiency can stop us from making our dreams come true.

I was majoring in Administration. Alert to everything that was going on, I heard about a multinational corporation that had opened a selection process for trainees. It was the position that most people at college coveted, you know? The topic always came up in the hallways: "I wonder who's going to get it?"

Everyone's motivation was simple: the position offered the best salary in the market.

In the wave of my classmates, I signed up for the selection process, submitting my academic resume.

I was always a great student within the standards of excellence of my time. My report cards were those that every parent would be proud to hang up on the fridge (In later years, my perspective of a 'good student' shifted, and now I disagree with the use of grades as a metric to judge a student).

A few days later, I received an email from the company.

From: Multinational Corporation
To: Rafa Brites
Subject: Invitation for the next phase of the selection process

You are invited to the next phase of the Internship Selection Process! During this opportunity, we will present the internship proposal and you'll partake in exams for general knowledge, logic, English (grammar and listening), Spanish (optional) and an essay.

Location: Fancy Hotel.
Note: Please bring a blue or black ballpoint pen and a calculator

So, I went again, this time in high heels, a blue button-up, and dress pants.

The project would be a competition between various groups, each one composed of ten people while four psychologists analyzed us.

One of them asked: "Who wants to be the leader of the group?"

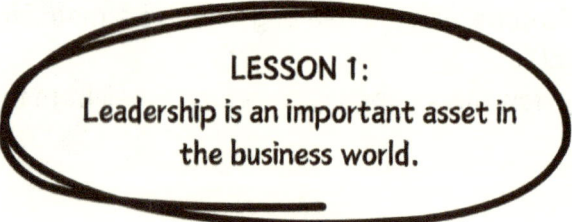

LESSON 1:
Leadership is an important asset in the business world.

I thought of saying: "Me!"

But, before I could say anything, three male colleagues jumped at the opportunity. The psychologist intervened:

"You all have to decide amongst yourselves who will be the leader."

The three of them, almost at the same time, pointed to each other and said, "Oh, ok. It can be him."

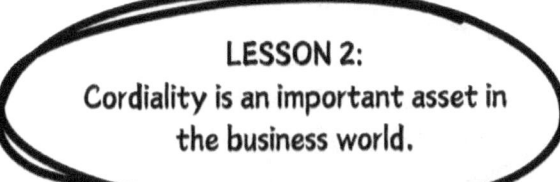

LESSON 2:
Cordiality is an important asset in
the business world.

So, one of the candidates said:

"How about we play Rock Paper Scissors to de-cide?"

Everyone agreed.

That's when I said:

"I don't think we should use luck or chance to de-cide on the leader."

LESSON 3:
Impartiality or justice is an important
value in the business world.

I asked the psychologist:

"Do we have ten more minutes?" She responded, "Yes, we do."

I proposed we all introduce ourselves. Since we didn't know each other, I suggested we all share what characteristics we had that made us good leaders and to share a short moment from our lives where we acted in a leadership role. At the end, we'd all vote.

LESSON 4:
Meritocracy is (or should be) the
foundation of the business world.

The psychologist wrote something down on her paper and smiled.

Point for me!

Everyone told a brief, but extremely heroic, story that demonstrated their leadership.

When my turn came, I felt the urge to say:

"Look, I don't really have a beautiful story like these. Actually, you can't really prove these stories that you just told, right? I'm the ONLY ONE here that has a story that can be proven, because I just convinced the nine of you to introduce yourselves and the four psychologists to give us an extra ten minutes."

Of course, I'd say all of that without being rude. In harmony (laughs internally).

So, I left it at that. Claim I'm a leader? Ew!

"Well, everyone, it doesn't really matter to me if I'm the leader."

Either way, what I did pleased those that were observing us.

Days later, a new email arrived:

From: Multinational Corporation
To: Rafa Brites
Subject: Invitational Email

Congratulations! You're invited to the Interview portion
of the Internship Selection Process!
There will be two interviews: one in Portuguese and one in English.

Location: The Multinational Company's Headquarters

The first interview in Portuguese went really well.

I was actually calm for the second part until I found out that it would be with the Mexican CEO responsible for the Latin- American branch of the company—in short, the most important guy in that entire building.

Ok, ok... Keep swimming...

I got there. The CEO was a man in his 50s, very kind.

"Hello, Miss Rafaella. How are you doing?"

"Hello, sir. I am fine, and you?"

"Blah blah blah." (Blá blá blá.)

"Blah blah blah."

"What do you think about the facilities here?"

...

I froze.

Facilities? What word is that? What are "facilities"? Is he asking me if I think this process is going to be easy?

I had no doubt:

"Excuse me. Do you mind if I search for something here?"

He laughed.

I swear on everything that is sacred: I pulled out my English-Portuguese dictionary (mobile internet search wasn't available at the time) and I searched *facilities*. Then I looked at him and said, in English:

"I'm sorry, I didn't know what *facilities* meant. I know I'm here to learn with you, but I will only ask questions that require answers I can't find somewhere else. Strategic questions. And yes, I loved the facilities."

Days later, I received the following email:

> From: Multinational Corporation
> To: Rafa Brites
> Subject: New interns integration
>
> Congratulations! You're now part of our team! We're counting on your presence at the 2007 Internship Integration Program.
>
> Location: Super Fancy Hotel.

I was selected from thousands of candidates—not just to be a company trainee but also to be the CEO's intern!

In other words, I didn't just get selected; I got selected for the best position of all!

Yayyyyy!
I got in!
Yayyyyy!
The CEO 's trainee!
I'm going to travel the world!

Ten seconds later...

WHAT?!
Me?
What do you mean?
Oh sh*t... What now?

My God, when I start the job "for real," they'll find out I'm not that good. They'll realize it was a huge mistake! That the other thousand were much better than me! That I don't know anything!

I don't know what the capital of Tunisia is. Actually, where is Tunisia? I don't know anything about geography.

I don't know anything about anything.

I was lucky to pass this selective process. I wonder if I won them over with my charisma. Maybe it was because I'm expressive?

Alongside this internal chaos, when the news spread - shocker! - I heard from some people this same sentence:

"Oh, of course, the CEO wants a hot female trainee to parade around airports like a luxury escort."

I'll confess that I'm tearing up as I write this. How could I hear this and stay silent? I wish I could go back in time and hold that Rafa in my arms.

(*Now's a good time to hug your pet.*)

And that's that.

I wish there was a better ending to this story, something like, "I turned things around and came out stronger. I believe in my potential. I started the job and was able to take care of everything. Today, I am the CEO of my own company." But that's not how it went.

From: Multinational Corporation
To: Rafa Brites
Subject: Admission Process - Documents

Hello, Rafaella!
I'm contacting you to request your documentation as without them we won't be able to continue your admission process. Please bring your documents as soon as possible to our headquarters.

From: Multinational Corporation
To: Rafa Brites
Subject: Admission Process

Good afternoon, Rafaella!
I tried contacting you this morning, but the phone number on file is disconnected. Please contact HR as soon as possible.

From: Rafa Brites
To: Multinational Corporation
Subject: Withdrawal

Dear Multinational Corporation,
I'm thankful for the opportunity. However, I will be moving to the United States in the coming days.

Sincerely,
Rafaella

I GAVE UP the position.

I was defeated by my insecurity. By my fear. By the feeling that I didn't deserve it.

My family that has always believed in me, didn't understand when I said that wasn't exactly what I wanted, which is why I was giving up.

"What do you mean you don't want it anymore? You were so excited!"

But, as always, they respected my choices and supported me.

The man who conducted my first interview called me and invited me out for coffee. He didn't seem to believe that I was actually going to move to another country. He kept saying:

"You have so much potential!" Your essay was wonderful. Your English is perfect!"

But NOTHING I heard on the OUTSIDE had any effect on the INSIDE.

Imposter! That's what you are, Rafaella Brites. An imposter.

RELAPSING IMPOSTER

In the ten years that followed, I lived with the same feelings on various occasions. Job interviews. Work meetings. Client visits. Project presentations,

It's not that I lacked self-love, but to me, I was always average.

And when I became a television host? Deceiving coworkers, bosses and pretending I had "more capacity" than I actually did was one thing. Bluffing on TV was another.

My God, a National imposter.

With millions of people watching, at some point someone would find out I was a farce.

The only thing that didn't add up was after living this way for years, my mask hadn't fallen yet.

What kind of luck is that?

How is it possible that there are so many polite people in this world telling me that I'm good at what I do?

One of these polite people was a director named Inês. I worked with her between 2016 and 2017. She'd look deep into my eyes and said:

"Fix your posture!"

"Why do you keep shrinking? What are you hiding from?"

"Speak firmly!"

"Believe in yourself!"

"Open that solar plexus and imagine there's a sun in there."

At one point, she said something that really stuck with me:

"Rafa, by not believing in yourself you don't share with others the best of you. That ends up being a form of greed. You're depriving the world of your qualities. You can make so many people's lives better with what you know how to do. But these people will never have access to that if you lock away your abilities because you don't think you're good enough."

Poooof! Mind blown.

My self-sabotage ended up being selfish.

So, I decided to dig deep and try to combat this imposter feeling that stopped me from being the best version of myself.

SCENES FROM THE MIND OF AN IMPOSTER #1

From the series "Really, you too?"

SHOW TIME

Now dear reader, picture yourself in this scene.

The theater doors open.

From the wings (of a stage) you can hear the voices of hundreds of people arriving to see the show.

YOUR show!

On this big, festive night, you're going to show what you do best.

The thing you've mastered in life.

That thing that's mixed into your personality, that's a part of your essence.

Beyond the voices, you notice the fragrance of the perfumes carefully selected by each one—the aroma of expectation.

The aroma is sweet and meant to emphasize the certainty that there will be a positive surprised. People arrive hoping to like what they will see. Others transpire a citrus aroma, refreshing, and meant to test you: "Surprise me if you can." They bet 50/50.

But there are those who stink of sulfur and came only to prove your own predictions of failure and lack of success. Their ironic smile is at the ready. They're just waiting for the right moment to use it, accompanied by the phrase: "I knew it would be bad."

From the edge of the stage, you see familiar faces: people you love and admire, friends, and family. Mixed in with them are strangers, people you've never seen.

Slowly, everyone finds their seat, filling each seat. It's a sold-out performance. The audience quiets down, the lights go out, and silence takes over.

It's your moment.

You're behind the heavy red velvet curtains, positioned at the center of the stage.
A single spotlight shines on you.
The show is about to begin.
Close your eyes.
What thoughts go through your mind?
What do you tell yourself?

Write down your thoughts here:

The bell rings, and the curtains open.

Maybe just by imagining this, you're already nervous, hands sweaty, having palpitations, stomach hurting, weak legs, and an intense urge to flee, to disappear, to disintegrate.

I don't know exactly what you wrote, but I am certain it WASN'T something along the lines of:

I AM INCREDIBLE!

I AM A BAD*SS!

I KILLED IT!

I AM THE BEST!

"Rafa, how did you know?"

From imposter to imposter: the first thoughts that pop into my mind are never those. My thoughts are more like:

WHAT AM I DOING HERE?

EVERYTHING IS GOING TO GO WRONG

THEY'RE GOING TO LAUGH AT ME!

I'M NOT THAT GOOD.

Relatable, right?

THE SECRET SOCIETY OF ANONYMOUS IMPOST-HERS

At this moment, you might be slightly shocked while thinking: *I thought this only happened to me.*

For years, I felt like an island, seeing so many women so sure of themselves. I imagined: How wonderful it must be to have the security of a famous writer with more than ten published books. How amazing it must've been when Maya Angelou finished a book, knowing she was already a renowned author, without this extreme fear of judgment.

So, I looked up how Maya Angelou felt after she finished each one:

"I have written eleven books, but each time I think, 'Uh oh, they're going to find out now. I've run a game on everybody and they're going to find me out."

- Maya Angelou

Hmm… Maybe she struggled with her self-esteem.

How about Michelle Obama? Yes. There's a strong, unshakable woman… I wish I was like her.

Let's get inspired by her.

Ladies and gentleman, a word from the former first lady of the United States:

"I had to overcome the question 'am I good enough'?"
- Michelle Obama

Oh, she's not as confident as I expected...

Let me think of someone who has been in the spotlight for some time... I know. Kate Winslet. She's a good actress: an Oscar, an Emmy, a Grammy, three BAFTAs, and four Golden Gloves... What a resume! Actually, when she received her third BAFTA she shared that at the age of 14 her theater instructor told her she'd only excel in performing arts if she were happy only doing "fat girl" roles - meaning no Rose in Jack's arms in *Titanic*.

Take that, professor.

How can she inspire us to be confident?

"Sometimes I wake up in the morning before going off to a shoot, and I think, 'I can't do this. I'm a fraud.'"
- Kate Winslet

Jeez. If the bajillion awards she's won aren't good enough, what would be?

It might be excessive rigidity on her part, and Brits can be a bit self-demanding.

Let's think of someone who has more in common with our culture. Like Jennifer Lopez, Latina goddess of pop music. She is a fearless, empowered woman. Who knows, maybe she can tell us the secret behind all that confidence?

"Even though I had sold 70 million albums, there I was
feeling like "I'm no good at this."
- Jennifer Lopez

Ok, ok. Seems like artists have very high standards. Let me see a different type of powerful woman. No
writers, or first ladies, or artists. An executive, who knows?
I thought of Sheryl Sandberg, Director of Opera-
tions at Facebook. She was the first woman to be nomi-
nated to occupy the company's board of directors. She
said:

"Every time I was called on in class, I was sure that I was
about to embarrass myself. Every time I took a test, I was
sure that it had gone badly. And every time I didn't embarrass myself — or even excelled — I believed that I
had fooled everyone yet again."
- Sheryl Sandberg

I GIVE UP.

What do you mean these powerful women feel the
same way I did at my internship?
Look at the resumes, fame, money, beauty, and
genius of these women. How could they feel this way at
the level they're on? Are they just being modest?
I don't think so. My first discovery brought me another, and
another... I kept finding these women saying phrases that
I would tell myself:

"Any moment, someone's going to find out I'm a total fraud, and that I don't deserve any of what I've achieved. I can't possibly live up to what everyone thinks I am and what everyone's expectations of me are."
- Emma Watson, actress, model and activist

"I still think people will find out that I'm really not very talented. I'm really not very good. It's all just been a big sham."
- Michelle Pfeiffer, actress and producer

"There are still days where something comes across my desk and I think, I don't know what I don't know about this. That is the scariest thing for me."
- Gwyneth Paltrow, actress and businesswoman

"You think, 'Why would anyone want to see me again in a movie? And I don't know how to act anyway, so why am I doing this?"
- Meryl Streep, actress

Maybe you're asking yourself why I, as a Brazilian, only chose quotes by non-Brazilian women. I did this to demonstrate that the feeling of incompetence, of not being good enough, is not solely related to local culture. It's very universal. And I confess that while reading these testimonials, I slowly felt some relief. I started to feel accepted as if I were at a secret support group meeting. I pictured myself in a large room where women from all corners of the planet arrive, take off their disguises and say goodbye to the masks they carry.

Meanwhile, they confess:
"I TOO FEEL LIKE AN IMPOSTER!"

Yes, reader. You. The person who has this book in hands and sees yourself within each quote: everything you have felt up until today is not exclusive to you.
You are not alone.

Welcome to

THE SECRET SOCIETY OF ANONYMOUS IMPOST-HERS
(SSAI)

HERE, GRAB A HANGER

Up until now everything seems so funny (maybe if you're like me and use humor to camouflage your insecurity). But it's not funny at all when you find yourself locked in your home bathroom, the office bathroom, a public bathroom, wanting to cry because...

... you felt incompetent.

... you get irritated when everyone lies, saying the opposite.

... no hairstyle, outfit, or makeup makes you less ugly.

... you have to swallow another frog because you're not going to find anything better.

... you believe everyone out there is better than you.

... you think you're easily replaceable.

... you believe you made it this far out of pure luck.

After crying you dry your face, touch up your smudged makeup, look in the mirror and say: "If you've pretended up until now, you can pretend everything is okay."

So, you put on a smiling mask and go out. Confident? Not at all. Determined? Just to survive one more day. Laughter is your weapon, the one you point at yourself: you laugh at your limitations, and joke about your fears. It's better to laugh than to cry, right?

Take off the mask, hang up the disguise. This is a sacred space where only the truth enters. If you don't know what the truth is, come in naked. Vulnerable. Exposed. That's how we all are, convicted imposters, although anonymous. No expectations. But full of hope.

We're waiting.

THE WAY OUT IS INWARD

The conclusion I reached, as I saw so many women underestimate themselves like me, is that this feeling is a reflection of a historical patriarchal construction. They are external factors that are abruptly reflected inside us.

In this book I'll talk about confronting the internal ghosts. But, beyond that, I'll demonstrate how it's important that we are ready and united to combat the origin of these ghosts, a more in-depth and systemic origin, caused by prejudices in regards to gender, race, class etc.

I'd like to emphasize that I write based on my point of view, from my personal reality. It'd be alienating and negligent for me to assume that all of us, Anonymous imposters, share the same story. Although, wherever you begin, when it comes to dealing with internal issues you can be sure of one thing while we seek external validation:

WE'LL NEVER BE GOOD ENOUGH.

The compliments, the diplomas, and the jobs will never fulfill the internal lack.

Thus, the idea that if we arrive at a certain level, the miracle of self-assurance will take over, is false.

I speak with authority as I understand myself to be a woman who has achieved many goals society puts on the recipe to happiness: money, fame, family, milk and honey... I have achievements that, for someone on the outside, would be more than definitive reasons for me not to question my self-worth. I'll say: personally, these achievements only added more pressure. And worse: the more I achieved and the better I did, the more exposed I felt and closer to the moment of being discovered as an *Impost-her*.

Looking back at my story and the stories of so many other women, I noticed that every step we take doesn't necessarily feed our self-esteem; instead, it seems like we become more vulnerable while the fear increases.

How have we fought this fear up until now? We've done loads of self-sabotage, self-boycott, procrastination, and self-deprecation...

Apologies for my frankness: we fight fear with cowardice.

But that changes when we understand that THE WAY OUT IS INWARD!

While we avoid diving deep inside of us and searching for the roots that cause us to have these feelings, we won't have the strength to combat the imposter that lives in us.

That is what I invite you to do in this book: understand *Impost-her Syndrome*, be alert, dominate it and be happy!

WHAT HAPPENS BEHIND THE MASK

THE PHENOMENON

Why is everyone always so confident, secure, and *chill* about what they achieved and didn't achieve, but I'm always afraid?

I'M NEVER ENOUGH!
I'LL NEVER GET IT!
I CAN'T MAKE MISTAKES!

Am I the only one?
I decided to do some research. Who knows, maybe someone who feels that same way has already found a way out and can help me?

My search led me to Pauline Clance and Suzanne Imes, psychotherapists and professors at the University of Georgia. During five years of private consultations, group projects, and classrooms, they interacted with over 150 super-successful women, academic doctors, respected professionals, and brilliant students.

However, they were united by one feeling: "I don't deserve to be here."

They didn't believe they were intelligent or truly capable. They believed that they occupied prominent positions by mistake (by the cosmos or themselves). In 1978, Pauline and Suzanne wrote an article about this feeling which they titled "The Imposter Phenomenon in High Achieving Women: Dynamics and Therapeutic Intervention."

"Dude, so much better than the title of my book..."

"Shhh, imposter! You're not going to get in my way this time! Go back to your corner!"

"But 'phenomenon' sounds so much better than 'syndrome'..."

"BLA, BLA, BLA! I can't hear you! La, la, la, laaa..."

Sorry for the internal discussion.

Where was I?

Oh, yes, Pauline and Suzanne.

So, they continued to study the imposter phenomenon and, years later, published a book on the topic.

Since then, many people have studied this syndrome. It's considered a universal problem as it isn't restricted to a certain age, gender, race, profession, social class, or other factor. However, it seems like it's stronger or more common within social groups with a lack of representation or that are in a disadvantageous situation.

Imposter Syndrome can't be detected through a clinical or psychological exam. It's not a disease or abnormality. It's more of a feeling we encounter in specific situations that are dependent on what we experience.

Everyone feels fear, anxiety or doubt every once in a while. The difference with imposter Syndrome is that it causes a cycle of constant shame and embarrassment, paralyzing the individual and leading them to doubt and question themselves all the time: *Do I really deserve this? Am I going to get that? Will I be able to handle it?*

How do we deal with it?

Although we will discuss this again later in the book, know that the important thing - actually the MOST important thing - is to admit that this is a problem.

The second most important thing is to inform yourself.

And the third is to talk about it (or write a book!). You're going to be shocked when you realize how common this feeling is. Actually, that's the idea behind SSAI: sympathize with people who have the same doubts as us. Share discoveries and create empathy. That way, we help one another tame this internal ghost.

ARE YOU A PART OF THE CLUB?

Do I have it?

Do I not have it?

Even though there is no exam, we can find out if there's an imposter within you.

Take a look at the scenarios below. They demonstrate the most common behaviors and thoughts of an imposter. Do you identify with some or even all of them? You may think the phrases below are too intense. Maybe you don't feel like that much of an Imposter.

For the purposes of this book, the situations mentioned are in the extreme. But they're not the rule. The Imposter can still be in there, camouflaged in your day-to-day behind a laugh and an achievement. Maybe even on days when you wake up feeling fabulous. This voice appears in the silence.

1. **You focus on the only thing that isn't perfect instead of looking at the 1001 that worked out.**

The Imposter easily takes care of five young children, but crucifies herself because she let the flowers in the bathroom window die. She chooses to pay attention to the negative (which it might not even be!) instead of focusing on the positive.

2. You think even a monkey could do what you did.

The Imposter thinks the things she does are sooooo simple. Anyone could do them. That's why she doesn't deserve compliments, admiration, rewards or recognition.

3. You believe something only has value if it's difficult.

The imposter thinks she doesn't deserve love, affection, sympathy, nor friendship unless she sweats through her clothes to get it. She often thinks: *No one would like me for no reason.*

4. You never do enough.

The Imposter has unrealistic expectations. She constantly compares herself to people who have nothing to do with her or sets standards that not even God could reach. And then she thinks that until she achieves this, she'll never be enough.

5. You value the imposter feeling.

The Imposter believes that she can't relax and that if she no longer sees herself as an Imposter she'll be "unmasked." On the other hand, if she continues to see herself as a fraud or a failure, it won't hurt as much when she "finds out it's true".

6. You're too busy feeling things.

The imposter focuses so often on your negative thoughts and feelings that there's no time or energy to execute things. While imagining that everything will go wrong, that she's not going to get it, that it's not going to work out, she ends up not even trying.

7. You only applaud others.

Finally, the imposter is capable of appreciating other people's journeys, seeing their growth and accomplishments. She can also see when someone has a huge positive impact on others—as long as that "someone" isn't herself. When the topic is the imposter herself, she becomes myopic.

WAIT A MINUTE, THIS DOESN'T HAPPEN

TO MEN?

How lucky to be a man and not suffer any of this.

It's not exactly like that.

Ok, maybe a little bit.

Men feel like imposters, but in a proportionally smaller number or degree than women, according to current research.

After many conversations with my husband, my male friends, and coworkers, I noticed clear differences between us and them.

Impost-her Syndrome	Rafa Brites
Think they're a bad*ss (as in badass).	Think they're b*d (as in bad).
Believe that success depends on **external factors**.	Believe that success is an **internal matter**.
Believe that they **already have everything** necessary for success	Believe they **don't have anything** they need to be successful.
When they succeed, they **believe they deserved it**.	When they succeed, they believe there was some sort of mistake because they **don't deserve it**.
If they're unsuccessful, they believe their skills haven't been discovered yet (**a lack of external perception**).	If they're unsuccessful, they believe they are not capable or hard working **enough**.

Of course, this doesn't apply to all men.

Studies show that there are men who feel like imposters. But most of these male cases occur within men who suffer racial and social oppression.

For example: a successful black man in a predominantly white environment or someone in a lower social class gaining prestige in an environment dominated by people in a privileged society. But what we can see in these studies (and even outside of them) is that women suffer more from imposter syndrome than men.

LinkedIn publishes a report about the impact gender has during a job search

For every **100** men who apply after seeing a position, only **86** women do the same.

68% of men ask for references from former coworkers, while only **32%** of women do the same.

Gender Insights Report: how women find jobs differently LINKEDIN.
Available at: <https://business.linkedin.com talent-solutions/resources/talent-strategy/ gender-balance-report>
Accessed on: 09/09/2020.

Why do women only apply when they meet 100% of the requirements?

According to research published in the Harvard Business Review, **22%** of women do not apply for a job position out of fear of failure. Only **13%** of the men interviewed have this fear.

Síndrome do impostor: por que tantas mulheres de sucesso se sentem uma fraude? PORTAL GELÉDES.
Available at: <https://www.geledes.org.br/sindrome-do-impostor-por-que-tantas- mulheres-de-sucesso-se-sentem-uma-fraude/>
Accessed on: 09/09/2020.

Paralyzed

The Imposter doesn't always show her face.

I don't always have my mask on.
I play with my son without a mask.
I talk to my sisters without a mask.

When I'm in an environment where I feel loved and safe, I am 100% in peace. I'm sure you also have many moments like this, mask less.

Generally, when we're comfortable, simply existing, as if we were the only people on the planet (or as if only the people we love lived here), the imposter goes to space. But then something happens and...

I... PARALYZE

Adiós, Rafa Brites!

Hasta la vista, self-confidence!

The imposter bubbles inside me and takes over everything.

After doing research to better understand what I had, I started analyzing what the syndrome represented to me. The first step was to identify the circumstances that provoked this self-perception of non-belonging and the sensation of being a fraud—the famous "I don't deserve to be here!"

I mapped out the paralyzation.

I saw that the word PARALYZE described exactly what I felt. On so many levels. It covered many scenarios. It's possible that you and I have some of these triggers in common.

Overexposure

In 2013, I had a surprise birthday party. I live in a house right off the street, you know how it is… I'm already a bit tense when I go to open the gate. When I arrived that day, the tension multiplied because I noticed everything was dark, and I always left the lights on (I always got the question: "Do you own the electricity company?").

I carefully went inside, shaking to my core. Until…

BOOOOOOOOOMMMMMMM!
(a huge explosion)

Tiny stars and confetti flew everywhere.
(Pay attention to the dramatic pause.)

I peed my pants.
(Please keep this information within SSAI)

At the biggest party I've had since childhood, I welcomed my guests with a puddle of pee.

I don't like birthday parties, but that's not why. It's because I get so embarrassed. I get the feeling that I'm bothering people. I typically go to everyone's birthdays, and I feel like throwing a party is an expectation. Maybe it'll rain. There will be a lot of traffic.

The thing is, I hate being the center of attention. I hate receiving presents and wishes of happiness. I hate hearing people sing "Happy Birthday to you" (and what do I do during that? Sing along? Just smile? Clap?). I love it when there's a child nearby because I'll grab them to blow out the candles and take the focus off of me.

Yes, being the center of attention is extremely vulnerable. When we are evident, like in a company meeting, we begin to think that at any moment someone is going to ask a question we won't know the answer to, and that is going to put all of our credibility on the line.

The feeling of overexposure multiplies on the internet. I have a friend, Tati, who, at some point, recorded a video about finances for women. When she went to see the results, she thought she looked fat and ugly. She shelved the project. One day, a year and a half later, she snapped out of it and decided to post the video. The video was incredibly successful. She helped thousands of women gain financial independence that day.

Because of this, I ask: in that year and a half that she didn't expose herself, how many more women could she have helped?

For fear of being evident, we can become selfish. To help others and change circumstances we have to expose ourselves. Show your face and speak to whoever wants to listen. I know sooooo many women make one, two, or maybe even three videos and find themselves terrible. They use phrases such as "Who am I to do this?" and give up. The result: everything stays the way it is. Or it gets worse.

Machismo

In 2009, I worked as a producer on a commercial set. My role ranged from arranging the food buffet to welcoming the cast. This activity required a lot of attention, especially time, because the set was rented, and everyone involved charged by the hour.

Despite that, sometimes the filming would get delayed. It wasn't always a huge problem, but it was tense when involving celebrities.

People are terrified of celebrities and their desires and habits. You never know if they're going to lose it when they hear that, unfortunately, the filming will go longer than expected. Being the one to deliver the news was like playing Russian Roulette, and it was up to me to give the news, especially if it was a man.

Because I was the intern? Because I could be diplomatic? Because I had tact? Maybe because it was my job?

No. It was because I had breasts.

"You go, Rafa, he won't get mad at you," my superiors would say.

It wasn't just with the celebrities. I was responsible for giving all updates to the men involved in the process.

I felt like a piece of meat being thrown to calm down the lion. That made me doubt why I was even there, my capacity, and everything else the Imposter keeps reminding us of.

For some, this task might seem like a compliment, but at the end of the day, situations like this really affect a woman's confidence in her own skills. The truth is that they discredit our abilities.

Sexist environments are always conducive to waking up the imposter. Women have to prove all the time that we're competent and that we're not there to just decorate the company meeting (yes, I've heard that before too).

The fact of the matter is that we're so calloused that we'll just throw on a fake smile. Or worse, we laugh and repeat the phrases to other women, which minimizes our strength. Think about it: when a woman receives a promotion from male superiors (because most continue to be male), there's a possibility they'll look at her and think, *"That one passed the couch test."* On the other hand, no man has his abilities questioned when he grows professionally.

In my opinion, systemic sexism is one of the biggest threats to our self-confidence.

Power

Prominent positions, from building manager to CEO of a multinational corporation, may seem highly coveted. But women who doubt their own capabilities think twice before accepting the position.

So many doubts start to come up:

Can I do it?

What if I make the wrong decision?

What if I'm questioned?

What if I upset someone?

I'll admit that I still don't know how to deal with positions of power, so I hire or associate myself with people who can perform in that position.

For mothers, there's also an aggravator: while we assume the multiple responsibilities power brings, we spend less time with our children and are judged for it.

I believe positions of power are especially challenging for women who have Imposter Syndrome because female leadership in the current capitalist society is something that is still in the crawling stages. Therefore, we try to reproduce the model of power traditionally associated with men: Aggressive. Cold. Relentless. Allow our emotions or sensitivity to come up? Don't even think about it. That's a weakness. A leader can't be serene, delicate, or speak softly—characteristics that are considered "feminine."

Wow, not even the angels get past that... They're all boys. I really wish there was a little Rafaella angel out there.

We believe leading means playing an energetic character, even if that isn't our style. We pretend we are like that. So as a result, what happens? We lose our identity and truly become frauds. In the meantime, we get extremely stressed and ask ourselves if we were ever the right person for the role.

As we reach a leadership post and continue to overthink about the situation, we create space for the *Impost-her*, to begin rambling and questioning the skills that put us there. We start to think that if we fail the whole world is going to find out.

They're going to start saying in the halls: "Did you see that? I told you so! She's not a leader at all. It was all luck". Just by thinking that our insecurity and anxiety build. At the first sign of questioning, we freeze and determine: "I wasn't born for this." In our minds, a leader is unquestionable. But we don't even stop to think about how many times we've questioned our moms, our dads, our teachers in school, our professors in college, our bosses, and the President.

Evaluation

There's a perfect occasion for us to have an existential crisis: during an evaluation. Exams, tests, applications, job interviews, electrocardiograms (Is my heart beating too much? Am I going to have a heart attack?). We are terrified of failing. I protected myself from this by studying more than everyone else (I think I still do this).

I remember knowing I had done poorly as soon as I completed a test. The day we'd receive the tests back was always the worst. When the teacher called me, I'd go to her desk with my eyes almost shut because I didn't want to see my grade. Heart beating fast. Hands sweaty. When I opened my eyes, I saw a 9.8 (out of 10) and thought:

Phew, how lucky am I.

When I was taking college entrance exams (we call it "vestibular" in Brazil), I was determined to enter a specific college for Administration. I was attending high school in the mornings, and I found a special study group that met up in the afternoons. It prepared candidates for ITA ("Instituto Tecnológico de Aeronáutica") and USP (Law School of the University of São Paulo)—the equivalent of getting into Harvard. We'd spend the whole afternoon solving almost impossible physics and chemistry problems that would never be on the exams I was planning on taking. But you know, I felt that if I wasn't prepared enough, I wasn't going to pass.

We think that's just childhood nonsense and that when we grow up, it'll pass. However, the same thing happens in job interviews, evaluations, and applications. I don't know if you've ever arrived for a job interview or an audition, seen the competition, and thought:

It's best I go home because I don't stand a chance.

Maybe you got up and left. Evaluation reveals another common type of defense for the Imposter: the famous "I didn't want it anyway." She doesn't want to fail. So when she sees a situation involving a possible rejection, she apologizes and claims that's not what she wanted. But it's not true.

The Imposter uses procrastination, lack of time, laziness, and lack of motivation to avoid confronting failure. We begin distributing this excuse to ourselves and others before the evaluation arrives. The person already thinks they're going to fail, so they think:

Why should I even try? Even if I study, I won't pass. I'm not going to waste my time. After all, they're all better than me.

And then she is paralyzed.

Confrontation

When I worked as a TV reporter, my experience allowed me to notice when certain things weren't going to work out. Most people who plan out the copy and the schedule don't experience the day-to-day life of being a street reporter. No problem; everyone's an expert in what they do. What should happen is an exchange of ideas and information—which the Imposter in me would rather avoid.

For example, there was a day when someone had the idea to ask people on the streets of São Paulo if they've ever cheated on their partner. Who was going to do the experiment? Me, of course.

On the inside I was certain that, for every ten people I interviewed, at least eleven would run away.

However, instead of communicating with the team and explaining how this could go wrong, I chose to move forward, waste a lot of time on the street, and have the film crew as proof that we tried, and it didn't work.

It was a huge nuisance, just to avoid the possibility of confrontation.

The Imposter thinks every exchange of ideas will turn into a battleground. And she fears that. She doesn't feel comfortable confronting because when she questions or confronts someone else's idea or position, she also becomes susceptible to confrontation. If that happens, it's over: she's going to be "unmasked." They're going to find out she doesn't have that many resources to defend her point of view...

So, I thought it was best just to stay silent.

Speaking for myself, a moment when I felt like the biggest Imposter in the world was when I had to share my ideas, critique or confront someone else's thoughts. As if in order to do that I had to be equipped with an arsenal of unquestionable arguments. Even then I was afraid of replicating.

The feeling of the Imposter in a debate is as if your mask is slightly loose. If the other person feels offended, they'll pull at you, and there you go. The world will find out who you truly are. They'll say you don't understand the topic, are a farce, or are delusional. And in case you get annoyed (#whohasn't, in the middle of a discussion?), you'd have to hear that you're "PMS-ing"...

Excuse me? Why did my menstrual cycle enter this debate?

We get offended by these things and agree that everything is true. We never stop to think that, maybe, who knows (laughs), you understand a bit more about the topic than the other person and that the true Imposter here is *her*, fearing she'll be discovered.

Come on, *Impost-her*, you think no one else in the world is an imposter?

Ascent

I got into *TV Globo* in July 2014. I was invited to cover the vacation time of a reporter colleague on the morning show *Mais Você*. They let me know very clearly that they weren't opening any new positions. It was just a substitute gig.

July ended and the other reporter returned. Sadly, I counted down the days until my contract, and my dream, ended. It was a mixture of gratitude and disappointment.

Two days before my goodbye, the director of the show called to tell me the wonderful news that they had opened up a spot for me. It was the best of both worlds:

I got in, and no one had to leave!

Months later, I received an invite to work on another show at the network, *Superstar*. It was a show about live music. As always, in the heat of the moment I screamed in the car out of happiness. But when it died down, the familiar sense of doubt started to creep in.

Why me? I'm such a newbie...

Do they know I don't have a journalism degree?

What about my other colleagues? Some have been there for ten years!

What if I'm not as good as the previous host?

And suddenly, this news that was supposed to be amazing became haunting.

Obviously if you saw me you'd have no idea that I felt this way inside. There's nothing like putting on our good old mask of "I'm doing great, thanks." Thankfully, more conscious of these imposter feelings, I accepted the role. In the end, everything went much better than I'd imagined.

For the Imposter, each step we climb increases the pressure. What for many would be a reason to celebrate, have pride, and give the ego a little massage, is a pit of concern for us, imposters.

The feeling is inversely proportional:

The more success, the less confidence.

That's why whenever we are promoted, approved, recommended, or selected, we feel like it's unjust to others. Someone in some corner of the cosmos deserved it more than we did. But deep down, this isn't altruism or modesty. It's the fear of not being able to handle it.

It's sad:

We fight so much for something, but when we get it, we can only think about how unprepared we are.

Recognition

To this day, I don't know how to handle compliments well.

Up until now, I've been able to map out two reactions I can have when receiving a compliment:

1. I don't believe what the person said.
2. I believe it, but I don't know how to react.

Whichever the reaction, I freeze up and start to stutter. Yes, I've learned not to apologize and to say "Thank you."

But I'll admit it's still very mechanical. Generally, I'll say it just to say it, not actually accepting what the person said. I think things like: *They probably don't really understand this if they're complimenting me.* The worst is when I try to prove to the person that there is no reason for compliments, I point out how I failed to do the right thing. How sad... I end up judging the sensitivity and capacity of someone else who just wanted to compliment me.

On the other hand, there's the feeling that if I thank them, I'll be agreeing with what they said, like a super polite way of being conceited, stuck up, arrogant. And suddenly the Secret Whistleblower of Anonymous Imposters, who's always lurking in every corner of the world, will jump out from the shadows and point the accusatory finger, saying: "Oh, so you think you're good, huh? Poor thing!"

So, to avoid that, it's best to respond to the compliment with self-deprecation.

If it's about my clothes, I diminish it by saying they were on sale, they're old, or they're borrowed.

If it's about my hair, I'll say I need a haircut, and I slept with it wet.

If it's about a cool attitude of mine, I'll say it's nothing.

And if it's about my career, I'll say it's just my job.

Believe it or not, the compliment I like to receive the most is that I smell good. In other words, something that only depends on a good, long-lasting perfume. Then I respond with a smile: "Wow, thank you!"

We can rarely be balanced and accept compliments with the same simplicity in which we'd receive a piece of candy someone offers us, unpretentiously.

The Imposter transforms the moment of a compliment into a huge event, like a test or an audit, when it should simply be an act of kindness.

Let's pause for a moment.

At this point, you might be a bit nervous, and we still have a lot to talk about.

Use the following page to express your artistic gifts

SCENES FROM THE MIND OF AN IMPOSTER #2

From the series "Really, you too?"

PMS

Premenstrual Syndrome

What is it?

1. "cyclical recurrence, during the luteal phase, of mood and behavioral symptoms, in the first instance, and somatic ones, with depression, anxiety, affective lability, tension, irritability, anger, sleep and appetite disorders being the most frequent."

2. "symptoms directly related to the phases of the menstrual cycle which can typically last from five to fourteen days. In general, they worsen as menstruation approaches and usually stop immediately or shortly after (one to two days) the beginning of menstrual flow."

But how is it utilized?

1. The key factor in disqualifying, devaluing or invalidating any opinion, feeling or more energetic positioning made by a woman.

A minute ago, I mentioned PMS, right? I felt like this topic deserved more space here. It's true that not every woman menstruates, but I bet they all know a woman that was undervalued because of PMS or their hormonal cycle, isn't that right?

I think it's unbelievable (or better, terrible) how much embarrassment women feel when it comes to talking about their cycles and fertility. The lack of conversation and information on the topic makes us treat this normal worldwide life event as taboo (yes, worldwide and not just women, because those who don't menstruate were born from someone that did). This isn't commented on, explained, or understood, so there is lots of room for ridiculous situations:

"Oh, we should talk another day. You must be PMS-ing," in the middle of a marital argument.

"Are you having one of those days?" when, for some reason, you're more emphatic in a meeting.

One time, a guy I had NEVER seen before cut the line at a concert. I yelled, "There's a line!" He turned around and said: "Calm down, I just came to talk to my friend. Control your PMS over there" I SWEAR! A complete stranger felt entitled to justify his bad behavior based on MY menstrual cycle.

We think PMS is only a current issue, but it's ancient! Some papyruses found in Egypt, written around

1500 BC, already spoke about diseases and disorders that affected women during their menstrual period.

I don't know how the Egyptians dealt with PMS without Buscopan. And I also don't know why, after so many centuries, this subject continues to be misunderstood and misinterpreted by both men and women.

Instead of educating, some women tend to imply that we agree with the stigma of hysteria and grumpiness that is tied to our menstrual cycle. That if a woman acts with energy, toughness and a dash of irritation (no one is made of iron), she is PMS-ing.

If a man reacts in the same way, what do they say? Probably nothing or "He's tough, right?".

The ignorance and misinformation around how the body of half of the world's population works puts women's capabilities into question, as if imbalance were a trait of feminine nature. Beyond that, it destroys female self-confidence and minimizes the situation that caused the stress.

Maybe I exaggerated?
Are my hormones controlling me?

As soon as the imposter settles in, you are no longer certain of anything.

HOW ADORABLE AND SO

WELL BEHAVED!

Pay attention to the families you know, especially the ones that have male and female children. How are the girls and boys stimulated? What is expected of each of them? What type of behavior is applauded?

For the boys, the typical compliment is: "This boy doesn't stop! He's such a little troublemaker. He climbs trees and draws on the walls. I don't even know how many times he's bumped his head. He's a lot of work!"

For the girls, the expected compliment is:

"Oh, what a sweet girl! She acts like a young woman. She's always quietly drawing. Your daughter is no work at all. She is so WELL BEHAVED!"

It's often heard that girls are easier to raise than boys. They're calmer, quieter, WELL BEHAVED.

When the girl is more active and less quiet, likes to climb trees and is not a big fan of playing with dolls, the commentary is: "This girl acts like such a boy."

I come from a family of three daughters. Meaning, we didn't have the gender comparison at home. But in the case of families with boys and girls, I know there is pressure, and that is a strong cause of imposter Syndrome. Women that have brothers feel like there was a higher demand to carry themselves in an exemplary way throughout their childhoods. Little quiet princesses, a trinket to be displayed in social gatherings. Pressured to be WELL BEHAVED. And it's not always the parents that induce this behavior, but uncles, neighbors, grandparents, teachers, acquaintances (the famous "Close your legs, girl!").

And when this girl grows up and doesn't feel so quiet and girly but she wants to compete in the UFC, drive a really powerful car or do anything society rules as more "masculine", she freezes. She feels like an Imposter in makeup and high heels, but also with her hands covered in grease.

Sometimes, the Syndrome has nothing to do with the fact that you feel incapable. It's just a matter of you not being yourself.

WHO SAYS?

Have you ever thought about the number of boxes you need to check off to be considered a successful "woman"?

o Menstruate by age 12.

o Decide on a college or university before 18.

o Choose your profession before 25.

o Be financially stable before getting married.

o Get married by the time you're 30.

o Have kids before 40.

o Have figured out the meaning of life before 50.

o Have a car, limousine, house, beach house, a house in a different country, a farm, private jet, yacht... and if possible, a rocket before 60.

And so on...

Did you feel the pressure? Exactly! We never stop to question these societal conventions that dictate the rhythm and even the priorities in our lives.

For example: why use high heels at a wedding knowing that at some point during the party you'll take them off and spend the rest of the night worried that you're going to step on a piece of glass or trip over the hem of your dress?

Huge problem, right?

What's the solution?

Wear different shoes?

No… Distribute flip-flops! (One more item the poor bride is going to have to worry about and spend a fortune on at a party that's already so expensive!)

Speaking of weddings, have you thought about why the father walks his daughter down the aisle to the husband?

In the past, and in some current cultures, a wedding was a financial transaction. That's why it was arranged - no one negotiated "out of love". The bride was "property," transmitted from the father's family to the grooms, and the dad took his daughter personally to the suitor, instead of "having her delivered," to make sure that the groom wouldn't back out at the last minute and ruin the negotiation. That's where the tradition of the father walking the bride down the aisle comes from.

Nowadays, at your wedding you're free to do whatever you want. Walk in with your father, alone… Who knows, you can come down in a spaceship!

The important thing is to do what makes sense to you and not the way it "has to be".

Who says?

Up until 1962 when the "Statute of Married Women" was promulgated in Brazil, married women could not vote, work, open a bank account, travel, or even open a business without her husband's authorization.

If no one had fought against these conventions, we'd still be living like that today.

So, thanks to whoever said "Who says I can't travel on my own?" because today women can enjoy freedoms that up until quite recently, weren't possible for our grand-mothers.

THE TERMINATOR OF THE PRESENT

A tendency I noticed during my Imposter Syndrome crises was my inability to live in the present. I was always thinking about the past or the future.

Sentences like these roamed my mind:

I should've studied so much more to be here.
Why was I in that relationship?
I won't be able to sustain this role in the future.

It was the **past** throwing around the **blame**, and the **future** bringing **anxiety**.

Obviously, it's important to evaluate our past and learn from it, or resignify it so we become stronger.

Thinking about the future is also inevitable, as long as it's done with precautions. A good example is to plan for retirement. But spending all night thinking about an inevitable upcoming flight isn't going to help us.

You know what's ironic? When we live in this altered space-time we use up all our energy. Then when H-hour arrives we've already been consumed by the past and the future. We're exhausted.

What if, just for a few moments, I was simply grateful for the here and now? What if I understood that the only moment that exists and that I can fully experience is this instant? It's everything that I have, everything I can truly change and everything that I can experiment with in every sense.

What if I was grateful for the resources I have, instead of focusing on what I lack (or on what I think I should have)? What if I was grateful for the opportunity **now**, instead of worrying about what is going to happen to it tomorrow?

When we're connected to the reality that surrounds us, nothing else matters. Neither what's passed, nor what's yet to come.

COMPARISON AND UNLOVE

The Imposter has a mother, and she is called *Comparison*.

With time we learn to unlove ourselves instead of doing the opposite. That's right! No one is born thinking they have a thousand flaws. We develop that as time goes by, and comparison has a fundamental role in this disservice.

Comparison is a human cognitive mechanism. Without it we wouldn't be able to go up or down stairs as we wouldn't have a reference for the height, size or distance. So it's impossible to say that at some point we'll stop comparing ourselves to others.

But there is a healthy way to do this: inspiration. Remember when you heard "If you want to be like them you have to…" or "They got a better grade than you?" All of these comparisons, initially harmless, leave deep scars on our self-esteem. This gets reinforced by "girl x boy" stereotypes, by the image of a "perfect" woman in the media, by the unattainable standards of success that lead you to compare yourself to what is considered ideal.

Comparison pushes us to focus on resources we don't have and we use other people's results as reference, eventually generating frustration within us. On the other hand, inspiration propels us to adapt our resources and learn from the path others have traveled to success, and that motivates us.

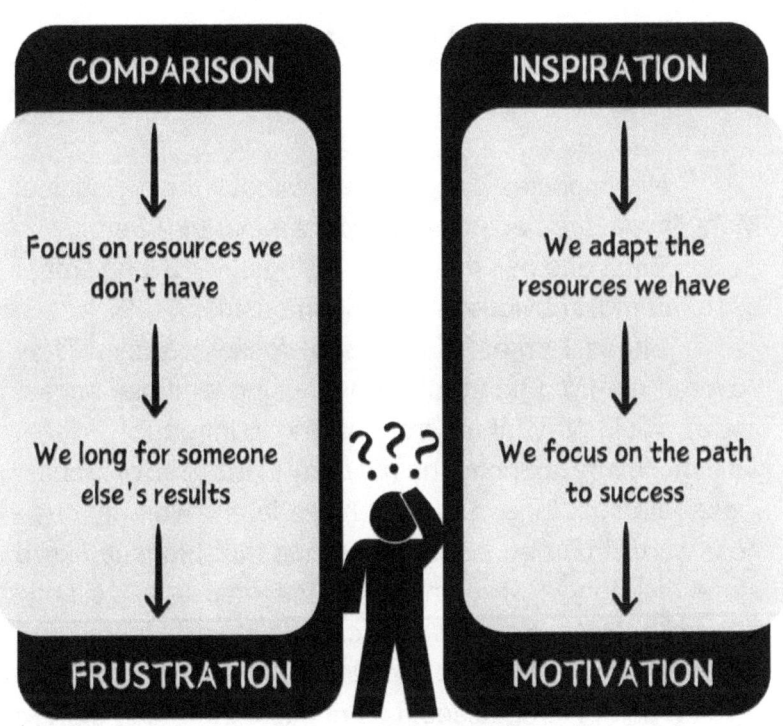

Think of someone who you constantly compare yourself to. Do the exercise of trying to shift how you perceive them: search for inspiration instead of comparison.

MY LUXURY DISGUISES

No imposter can do well without their disguise. Many layers are necessary to conceal our true Self.

Each one has their own strategy. For a long time, I used the most obvious one: consumerism.

Shoes. Purses. Sunglasses. Jacket. Jewelry. They covered me from head to toe as if using all those accessories would prevent me from having to introduce myself. As if the luxury imprinted on my body in the form of fabrics, logos, stamps, tags, and expensive labels was my business card. I carried so many brands that I looked like a store directory. But in my mind the message I silently transmitted was: *See, I'm successful! Power! Money!*

One day, I went to the mall with the prescription for my first pair of eyeglasses. I went into a store and started trying on all of the different options. Dior, Fendi, Tiffany & Co. with a teal frame, Chanel, Prada... with prices were around $300, $800. Until:

"Wow! I love these. What brand is it?"
"It's called Charm."
"Charm what? What's the brand?"
"Just Charm. It's a Brazilian brand. It costs $40."

Upon hearing the cost, I immediately let go of the frame and continued my search for the perfect glasses while deep in my brand "blindness". I tried all of the frames in the store, but none of them fit as well as the ones from

Charm did. But how was I going to participate in an important meeting without my disguise? Without my glasses of success that prove I won in life?

Some stores later, I walked out of the mall thinking about the $ 147.00 glasses. I went home bothered. At home, I had one of those moments of clarity where we question the standard we follow blindly. The famous "Who says?"

BOOOOOOOM! Mind blown!

My God! I was tricked!

I went into my closet and noticed everything I had accumulated. Each piece I had purchased. Each moment I wasted inside a store during my travels. It made me sick, followed by a feeling of a lot of self-pity. What is this emptiness that I keep trying to fulfill by shopping?

I closed my eyes and asked myself:
What is success to you, truthfully?

Many answers came to mind: contribution, purpose, peace, fulfillment. None of them were connected to ostentation. I won't lie, there were moments where using red bottomed shoes and a purse with an original gold chain gave me the sensation of security. But where were my greatest riches: simplicity, humility and a beautiful captivating smile?

Probably crushed by the red bottoms or tied up in the chains.

After this epiphany of thoughts and memories, I went back to the mall the next day and left with my beautiful pair of Charm glasses and the lightness of having saved some money,

I cleaned out my closet. I donated two Hermès Birkin bags (let's not comment on the value of that bag). I sold everything that I only loved because it represented my achievements.

Years have passed. Today if you run into me, you can be sure that the last thing that will catch your eye is something that was purchased. Actually, I notice that other women have gotten a lot more comfortable with my presence once I abandoned my disguise.

LOVE PEOPLE AND USE THINGS.
THE OPPOSITE WILL NEVER MAKE
YOU HAPPY.

I still use my Charming glasses. And now I can actually see you too.

ATTENTION:

I DON'T REPRESENT EVERYONE

When Imposter Syndrome was "discovered", it was initially detected in a small controlled group. There's a reason why the title of the article written by Pauline and Suzanne is:

PSYCHOTHERAPY: THEORY, RESEARCH AND PRACTICE VOLUME 15, # 3 , FALL, 1978

The Imposter Phenomenon in High Achieving Women: Dynamis and Therapeutic Intervention

Pauline Rose Clance
Suzanne Ament Imes

In other words, the initial research group consisted of women who in one way or another was considered successful.

But more recent research on the topic shows that Imposter Syndrome isn't exclusive to successful people, people in high positions, and not only women. It is "democratic" (just like Brazil, haha): it can hit any person with difficulties in belonging. Because actually, the world is not yet "democratic." Quite the opposite: it is still unjust, prejudiced, unequal and cruel.

What happens is that this feeling of displacement doesn't translate in the same way for everyone. So, what I share here refers to my reality and the type of woman I represent: white, privileged, and I most certainly having made many racist and classist mistakes in my interpretation. I apologize for that. (By the time this book is circulating I would've read more books and taken more lessons out of the pages of bell hooks as I'm in eternal deconstruction.)

Each group – actually, beyond that – each INDIVIDUAL will feel the Syndrome differently.

In my path of research and discoveries I noticed my perception is only a small piece. Which is why I invited some dear friends to share how they experience Imposter Syndrome, each one in their own skin.

"I have always been a creative person. My family discovered this when I was still very little. I woke up each day being something different: pianist, truck driver, dentist, tie seller, Olympic swimmer... Everything I did was with unquestionable conviction. But then I grew up, and only in adulthood did I discover myself as a black woman. This process of becoming aware of my black identity came with baggage, and one of the burdens was Impostor Syndrome. The myth of racial democracy denies racism in Brazil and thus questions my blackness because I am a light-skinned black woman. Every day I question myself on my lack of legitimacy, about my lack of sufficient theoretical foundation, about my role as a social educator. Impostor Syndrome is a reality for many women, but with the intersection of racism, everything weighs at least twice as heavily on the body, heart, and conscience of a black woman."

- Debora Bastos, social educator

"Society is not prepared to professionally assess people with disabilities. This is my reality, which forces me to look for tricks and, sometimes, to be an Imposter in order to prove my competence, my talent, and my intelligence. In the artistic world, where there are expected standards for height and beauty, sometimes I find myself forced to send my materials saying that I am 5 ft tall, which is not true since I have dwarfism (4 ft). But if I don't do it this way, when will I have opportunities? So, this is me: my name is Juliana Caldas, and deep down I know that my ability is much greater than my height. But unfortunately, I consider myself a 5-foot tall Imposter because I need to create job opportunities."

- Juliana Caldas, actress

"I remember when I was young and I still didn't have an ID that matched who I actually was. It also didn't have the name I chose to have. So I had to make a fake one. Yes, I got a fake ID. Is it wrong? Is it a crime? Yes! But I would rather be arrested for 'ideological falsehood' than go through the embarrassment of being addressed by a male name. Nowadays, the scenario has changed a lot. We have climbed a few steps, but we are still far from the 'ideal'. The LGBTQIA+ community, especially the trans community, is still marginalized and often the target of bad jokes. A few years ago, I was able to exchange all my documentation; at the time it was the first case in which the certificate said 'female sex' without any mention of being trans. It was something unprecedented and opened jurisprudence for future cases. It was an advance. In fact, being alive at 40, being successful and having a 'normal' life is a victory, considering that the life expectancy of a trans person in Brazil is 30 to 35 years. Our country holds the record for homicides against transvestites and trans people in the world. Even though I am seen by everyone as an unshakable fortress, only I know of the many moments when I felt like an Impostor. Even being the positive woman that I am – because I believe that we cannot give problems more weight than they actually have –, there were moments when I almost broke down. But I persevered!"

- Carol Marra, actress and journalist

"I was 13 years old when I received a scholarship to a private school. At the time, I spent a whole year having nightmares where the school regretted giving me the scholarship and I went back to studying at a public school. I was 18 when I was accepted into Harvard, also on a full scholarship. I thought this dream was so unattainable that I asked the person responsible for breaking the news to me if that call was a prank call. When I lost my father to drugs, four days after my acceptance to Harvard, I believed that I had really taken a step beyond my reach. I only said 'yes' to the university weeks later, at the encouragement of my teachers, who were unable to convince me that I could handle the challenge, but who made me see that it could be many years before another student from the ghetto would have the same opportunity. In my first year at college I was sure that I would never learn English and that, eventually, everyone would realize that I wasn't that good. Six years later, my fight for education led me to run for the position of federal deputy. On election day, once again, it took me a while to believe that I had actually been elected. I'm still learning how to deal with attacks, threats and attempts to disqualify me. I strive to remind myself daily that they have nothing to do with my ability, but rather with machismo, which tries to convince us that, in my case, a woman's place is not in politics. Sometimes, I can't do it and, even if only for a short time, I question whether I should even be here, until I realize that the best answer I can give is to transform my fear and insecurity into a fight, so that other women can also take their place."

-    Tabata Amara, political scientist

It's impossible for me to not be moved by the words of my dear friends, and not notice that even inside this vast Secret Society of Anonymous Impost-hers there are abysses created by prejudice and racial and social stigmas.

SAYING GOOD-BYE TO THE DISGUISE

TIME TO SHINE

Well, my dear disguise partner, I know life united us through these words and confessions, not chance. I would've liked it if we had recognized the Syndrome beforehand, if we had been warned about her in school or when we already didn't believe we belonged.

What we've lived up until now is part of our story. With her, we became calloused. Sometimes, it feels like there's a knot in my chest, a disappointment when I realize that there are so many layers to be undone before we arrive at our true Self, that we can only change by being born again. To be secure. To own yourself.

Unfortunately, I can't claim that I've found the definitive cure. Something that annihilates the imposter.

BUT, YES! It's possible to fight her or, better yet, welcome this woman that is exhausted from fighting so much external and internal pressure. Embracing her is possible.

The first step is being aware that she exists, to have the diagnosis that she is inside you (at this point, I believe that has already happened).

Now we will talk about how we can make this shift, this new beginning of embracing our real identity. How to say goodbye to the disguise. And have no fear.

IT'S TIME TO SHINE.
(I just got butterflies!)

Enough

The first step after seeing yourself within so many characteristics of the Syndrome is to decide that you don't want to be paralyzed anymore. It's to promise yourself you will be attentive to each and every trigger that can make the imposter take over.

It takes courage because the feeling of exposure when we decide to walk around without our disguise isn't so "I'm free!" in the beginning. It's like being naked.

We'll miss the armor, the withdrawal, the procrastination. The things that bring us psychological protection.

We believe that the feeling of insufficiency and inability is tied to what others think of us. But it is, above all, the result of what we think of ourselves. So, before we introduce ourselves to the world we have to know who we are.

The path of self-knowledge is the first chapter in any transformation. Yoga, meditation, Freudlan therapy, Lacanian, behavioral, reiki, coaching, Access Consciousness Bars, TSER by Rafa Brites (I highly recommend). The method that leads you to believing in your potential doesn't matter. When you believe that you're capable and interesting then you'll be offering the world the best version of yourself.

And criticism? Oh, yes, it'll always come. But instead of penalizing and beating ourselves up about it, we'll first consider it. If we feel like it offers us an opportunity to improve, to evolve, that's how we'll perceive it. Failure is an opportunity to progress.

Living in a state of alert is important. When we put an end to our inner deprecating voice, when we understand it and substitute it for a welcoming and motivating voice, we begin to trail a wonderful path. With no return.

Reconnection

Imagine an alien spaceship lands on your street. An army of aliens à la *Alien vs Predator* come out of it, armed to the teeth (which are also weapons). They knock on your door and in a hollow, robotic scratchy throat voice say: "We've come to exterminate all of humanity... Argh... Except for those that have something to teach us".

What would you do? How would you save yourself?

I'm sure you'd make up something to save yourself. "Look, I know how to do jumping jacks! I know how to tie my shoes! I know how to act like a statue until you all go back to the hole where you came from!"

We have the bad habit (or maybe it's an addiction?) of only paying attention to the things we're not good at or need to develop. We end up forgetting the things that we're good at.

It's important to reconnect with your story and your talents to rescue your worth.

I believe we lose the connection when we learn to compare ourselves. Then we establish standards that don't reflect who we are.

I won't be a hypocrite and say that life is always rose colored. But I want to encourage you to seize your life and your past.

Get on that unicorn and let's go!

I don't know your past. But I know that no matter how crazy some moments may have been, you can look back at them with a certain distance and give them new meaning. I don't mean "erase them" nor "belittle them", but understand what the lesson was.

Our story makes us unique. It gives us wisdom. And wisdom doesn't just come from getting a postgraduate degree, being a PhD or staying up all night studying. Wisdom also comes from experience. When we disconnect from our origins we also leave our knowledge behind.

You won't be fulfilling your purpose until you reconnect with your story and recognize your singularity and value. Until then you'll get frustrated for trying to fit into a space that is someone else's.

Your beauty and value are in your singularity and not in how hard you work or how much you dedicate and commit. While you don't accept yourself and dive deep into who you are to bring out your potential, you'll always be a forgery of someone else.

And the whole world misses out.

Information

Information liberates us and opens up paths towards change. Studying our history is fundamental to understanding the reflection it has on society and in our lives. Unfortunately, not everything we learned in school is the truth. The history we learn (in current teaching standards) is narrated from the point of view of white, cisgender, straight men and almost always stemming from rich families.

Or do you still believe that Brazil was discovered by Pedro Álvares Cabral?

We grow up without an education on our ancestry, disrespecting and massacring many people, and even committing cultural appropriation. Those who don't understand where they come from will hardly be able to understand where they are (a fertile field for an imposter, huh?).

Get informed. Read books (a point for you as you are already doing this). Seek alternative versions of facts that are apparently "settled". Search for testimonials of other imposters that let their masks fall and learn from them.

Get inspired by other people's stories to write your own, reach your own conclusions and create your own strategy.

And be careful with the information you consume.

- Good information allows us to walk on our own two feet. It can be free or paid, but it empowers us to create a strategy, instead of making us dependent on method X or Y, gurus, or even real imposters (the world is full of them!).

- Don't look at the testimony of other women as the only sacred path to follow. Each person deals with the Syndrome in their own way. Instead of comparing yourself, be inspired by them.

- Don't make information, or the lack thereof, an obstacle to shining. Read and study in the amount that is possible for you. Work with the resources you have, rather than putting it off until the day you feel properly equipped (trust me, that day will never come!).

Fight

Maybe "Fight" isn't the cutest word when it comes to shining. But it's a part of it. From what I know, no change comes without confrontation (which is not a problem for us at this point in the game, right?).

There is an individual and internal fight that combats the effects of imposter Syndrome. But there's another more comprehensive one that will combat the CAUSE of this Syndrome.

For example: what's the point in carefully hanging your clothes on a line if a storm comes soon and ruins everything? You need to build a roof to protect your clothes that are on this line. You need to change the ENVIRONMENT.

Our fight is to change environments and situations that generate and proliferate the imposter Syndrome. We have to build an atmosphere where no one feels the need to mask themselves as an imposter in order to feel capable. That involves small actions - such as not laughing at a sexist joke in a work meeting up to movements that advocate for the increase in the number of women in political positions. The fight also requires historical reparations through antiracist and inclusive actions.

I am someone who has rarely made categorical statements. But, if I'm certain of anything, it's that the revolution (that our world desperately needs) will come from us, women, mothers, daughters, partners, professionals, citizens, because in the fight for a better world we won't be silent in the face of injustice. Are you in this fight with me?

Habit

I also call this "being on the lookout". Today I am someone who is always there, hiding in the bushes, ready to fight back when imposter thoughts come up.

Personally, I don't believe that there's a cure for imposter Syndrome (don't get discouraged, there's a BUT). But, it can be controlled, like high blood pressure or diabetes, so it doesn't present more risks to your mental and emotional health.

The secret is in the HABIT.

Think about it: with the Syndrome we have the habit of questioning other people's intentions, our capacity, our achievements. It isn't a behavior that appeared out of nowhere. We trained it to do this, and today we repeat this behavior automatically.

So, it's totally possible for us to educate our internal Self, that voice we talk to all the time, to have more healthy and constructive habits.

Here are some good habits you can put into place now:

- **Monitor your thoughts.** It's about leading yourself.

- **Identify obstacles.** I shared with you earlier when I talked about paralyzing, the things that wake up the imposter and make me feel like a fraud. Maybe we have some points in common. Maybe not. So, evaluate yourself: in which situations do you start to question your value, your achievements? Is it in the presence of certain people? Is it when you are in specific locations or appointments?

- **Prepare strategies to deal with obstacles.** If necessary, put together a "tactical notebook" and carry it with you. For example: I feel like an imposter when I go speak at a big event – and I feel even worse when I know that there is someone in the audience that I really admire. My strategy during these times is to pause a few minutes beforehand and think: *I came here to share what I learned. My own story, my own discoveries.* I start to calm myself down. Not that I don't get nervous when I pick up the microphone, but I no longer feel like the Imposter of the night.

- **Visualize success.** Professional athletes often visualize themselves crossing the finish line. Do this before a tense moment. Imagine giving the best talk of your life, being hired, leading your team with ownership. This will reduce your stress and make you think: *Hey, why not?*

- **Reward yourself.** Praise a job well done. Celebrate an achievement. Don't wait for praise or recognition to come from others. Give yourself the honor of being the first person to congratulate yourself.

Acceptance

You know that friend who you can count on at any moment? That's always willing to raise the vibe when you are low?

Well can you imagine yourself going to this friend after she's ended a relationship and saying: "Well, you aren't that interesting"? Or, after she had a bad day at work say: "Wow, you're actually lasting at that company..."?

NEVER!

We never treat the people we care about like this. But why do we do this to ourselves?

Why do we expect so much from ourselves? Why are we so cruel to ourselves, especially when we're vulnerable?

Now imagine living with an enemy like that for 24 hours a day, by your side. Actually, not by your side, no! INSIDE you! It's so much worse.

Do you see how the conversation we maintain in our mind is toxic and humiliating?

We grow up learning to speak to others in a polite way: "Thank you", "Please". We learn to compliment and to offer help. There's no way you wouldn't say "Thank you" when someone brings you a glass of water, right? So I ask you: when was the last time you thanked yourself or said "Please" to yourself?

We're illiterate (that's right, we're unable to read and write). We NEVER learned to communicate internally in a generous and compassionate way. We didn't learn to embrace the internal Self that is upset, grieving, embarrassed, lost...

Every once in a while, stop in front of a mirror and offer yourself a smile, who knows maybe even a wink, without noticing if your skin is bad or if you have bags under your eyes.

You can argue saying they're just "thoughts". I'll respond with the quote I heard from my dad my whole life:

"Watch your thoughts, they become words;
watch your words, they become actions;
watch your actions, they become habits;
watch your habits, they become character;
watch your character, for it becomes your destiny."
- Frank Outlaw

Support System

I lost it when I found out Michelle Obama felt the same way I did.

I felt so close to her!

Honestly, as I spoke about imposter Syndrome and my feelings many people said: "Wow, Rafa, I feel the same way!"

When we find the courage to open up and share how we feel, people start to relate. You realize you're not the only one who doubts themselves. With that, instead of feeling excluded and displaced, you see yourself as part of a huge cross-cultural, welcoming community:

The Secret Society of Anonymous imposters.

Breaking the silence and exposing your feelings is liberating. If we don't communicate we won't uncover the challenges or the stories of the people around us. In the same way we don't speak on our own challenges or our own story. This "unfamiliarity" creates a favorable space for comparison and judgment - triggering situations that ruin us. But when we create a support system, when we're honest about our feelings and are open to listening, understanding and embracing the feelings of others, there's no reason to use masks.

Talking about imposter Syndrome and being honest about your feelings is, to this day, the most accurate way to deal with the feeling of being a fraud. Which is why, all of us Anonymous imposters, need to be willing to break the silence and create support systems around us.

As in any community, you need to be ready to offer support in addition to receiving it. Keep an eye out for the paralyzing triggers, and many others, that might strike the women around you (men too, poor things). Be this force for the people closest to you.

As I've mentioned before, here we deal with internal issues that are a reflection of many external issues. And we can make a difference. As citizens, we can fight for ALL women. Within our gender there are still social and racial gaps that need to be repaired. We can make changes in our daily lives, but beyond that, the change MUST be systemic. *But how?*

In my opinion, politics is the best tool to make this happen. Come on, Rafa, you're delusional, right? Politics? I hate politics.

To that I say: you might be disappointed because you don't feel represented. In Brazil female representation in civil positions is minimal. We make up more than 50% of the population and don't occupy even 15% of elected positions.

Our role as a support system is to also be a driving force. We can encourage women to run for office, combat Imposter Syndrome (imagine how hard it hits)... Push for equality in races, in campaign financing and, of course: vote for women. Black, white, trans, lesbian, people with disabilities...

So, strengthen your network. You can start by recommending, gifting or passing on this book (just don't photocopy it).

You'll probably be surprised, like I was, when you realize that our Secret Society of Anonymous imposters is much bigger than you imagined.

APOLOGY LETTER

On the other side of the support systems are the judgments we make of other women. A historical hatred stimulated by the false idea that we, women, are rivals. I try to free myself from this harmful feeling, to support more and more women.

One of these days I wrote this letter of apology, to remember the moments when I failed. I invite you to reflect on this and, perhaps, even write your own.

I'd like to apologize.

Sorry for thinking you wanted to steal my boyfriend, mislead me at work, take my position, or occupy my space.

Sorry for gossiping about your life. For calling you fat, skinny, desperate, a groupie, a gold digger.

Sorry for saying you purposefully trapped him with the pregnancy. Such an ugly thing to say, right? I'm ashamed of that.

Sorry for not defending you when MEN at a bar called you a tramp. Even worse, I probably laughed along.

Sorry for calling you names just because you were an ex. Or for judging you for being with someone who was in a relationship. As if the guy has no blame, poor thing! I don't even know if you were suffering or if you were deceived. Nonetheless, I judged you.

Sorry for pulling up a picture of you just to look for flaws. It's because you looked so beautiful, there just had to be something wrong. I was taught that we are rivals, competitors. Not from my household, because in there we come in three incredibly united sisters. I have many girlfriends. But you're not in my family or friend group. You are that other woman.

I apologize for the times I dismissed an achievement of yours claiming you used other resources that don't include your intelligence or merit. I said that you were probably someone's daughter or you took the couch test. I was so immature when I said that. I would never do it again.

Sorry for not getting close to you, and for stopping you from getting close to me. Or for pushing you away. When women turn away from each other, they turn away from who they are. We turn away from our nature, our power, our strength. They made up this whole competition and rivals thing to weaken us. And it truly weakens us so much! No one wins this fight. Everyone suffers!

Maybe all of this was said about me too. And so, we never got close.

I hope you can forgive myself.

SCENES FROM THE MIND OF AN IMPOSTER
REHAB

From the series "I've seen this film before"

"NO" IS A COMPLETE SENTENCE

One of the biggest difficulties an imposter has is denying something to someone. As always, we need to feel like we have gone above and beyond. That we tried harder. We become more available than we should be.

Saying "No" is almost an impossible task.

We become overwhelmed, taking on much more than we are capable of. We tried our best not to say "No" (even when, internally, we brooded and cursed ourselves for knowing that the right thing, once again, was to not give in).

When we occasionally catch our breath, take a deep breath and manage to say no to something, it's always followed by a justification.

"I CAN'T GO BECAUSE..."

And we explain ourselves. We say we have no time, no money, no childcare and so on. With each explanation we give the other person opportunities to offer solutions and options that make us change our mind, until it becomes too inconvenient to say "No".

"OH, CAN'T YOU LEAVE HIM WITH YOUR MOTHER?"
"TAKE A TAXI!"
"OPEN A CREDIT CARD."
"WE CAN SPLIT THIS AMOUNT BY 900."

But I want to say one thing: **"No"** is a complete sentence.

Beginning, middle and end: it's all in there.

Of course, we don't want to be rude, but it's just saying: "Wow, unfortunately I can't this time". Period. (You might need to practice a bit in front of the mirror.)

But that's it. Don't know how to say "no"? Just say it. (You've already said it to yourself so many times...)

I CAN'T.

I'M NOT AVAILABLE.

I DON'T NEED IT

THANK YOU, BUT NO.

CAREER TRANSITION

So, what are you going to be when you "grow up"?

I'm sure you've heard or asked this question at some point in your life. The answer to this question is normally based on things we enjoy, or on the profession of someone we admire. We want to be veterinarians because we like animals, or TV hosts because of Xuxa (or Ana Maria Braga in my case). There's a chance we'd want to be an engineer or work in administration because our mother's or really cool uncles did.

Everything is easier when we're kids, of course. But then we get a bit older and adolescence arrives with a whirlwind of emotions. The time to decide is approaching and the confusion in our minds only grows.

At around 17 you need to know what you're going to do professionally for the rest of your life (as if that were possible). You need to know what you do best, what you like, many times without even knowing what half of the possibilities are. Doesn't that seem a little crazy to you? To me it is!

In my case, at that age, I decided to follow in my dad's footsteps. He's a businessman. But you know what he majored in? Veterinarian medicine and Law. You see what I mean, right?

If we go back in time, centuries ago people practically didn't even have the option to choose their careers. In a family of shoemakers, the children would most likely become showmakers. Those that departed from the family tradition were seen as rebels, simply for desiring something different. As time went on and industries developed, working at a large company became the dream for many young adults. The civil service positions... Woohoo! Those who were approved were the family's pride.

However, everything changes. I've worked in many places, some for more time than others. Life is like that now. Evolution brings changes in thoughts, opinions, desires. New professions appear while others are extinct.

The Economic Commission for Latin America and the Caribbean (ECLAC) released some interesting data: around 65% of students who are in basic education at this moment, will work in a profession that doesn't exist yet! Woahhh!

There it is. The profession wasn't even invented yet.

Specialists show that even though the future of work will be technological, human skills will be valued the most. We will be extremely necessary in areas where robots cannot reach.

But let's say you do as I did. You muster up the courage and decide to change your profession. You decide to face the big "career transition". That moment in which we're still starting in a new industry, with the impression that the whole world is watching us looking like "huh": "Didn't you study business administration? What are you doing on TV?", "Weren't you a TV host? Why are you teaching self-discovery classes?". And so on.

I know so many people carry the fear of change.

What I have to say to them (and to you) is that no one changes careers!

What?

What do you mean?

Yes! A career is everything you build throughout your life. When we change professions, we don't delete what's been lived. On the contrary, we carry some lovely baggage that I divide into 5 C's.

Cultivation

It's everything we've learned in contact with one another, all of the exchanges made with people around us. When we start at a new company or change our profession, we bring with us all of the knowledge we've cultivated throughout the process.

Contacts

This includes all of the people you've met, the partnerships you made and the support systems you've created throughout your career. Each person that comes into your life is important to your professional and primarily your personal growth.

Coin

Those who work want and deserve to be compensated. The coin is the money you are receiving from your work, or what you are able to save. It's important to evaluate if what you are receiving is compatible with the role you are performing, and if it's enough to supply your needs.

Contentedness

It's having pleasure in what you do. Going to work every morning is not always easy (there are days where we just want to stay in bed all day!), but when we enjoy being where we are and performing our role with a greater purpose, the effort is gratifying. That's contentedness!

Contribution

How is your work contributing to other people's lives and what kind of value does it generate? Think: is your craft making a difference in the world?

DON'T BE AFRAID OF CHANGE!

The world won't stop and wait for you to feel totally safe.

WHAT'S IT WORTH?

If you, reader, suffer from Imposter Syndrome, I know one of your main struggles is knowing your own worth. Your innate worth. Giving importance to yourself.

This is reflected when it comes to charging a monetary value for your service.

We're screwed!

What I often see are women saying they don't know how to charge for the work they do. Makeup artists, hairdressers, lawyers, dentists. It doesn't matter. The truth is that there is this feeling that if we increase the price no one will pay. Or worse, they will say:

"Who does she think she is to charge that?"

I know cases of friends of mine who often ended up paying to work. That's right. What they charged did not even cover the costs of the service.

And asking for a raise at a company? Just thinking about it gives me a stomach ache.

It's as if by setting a lower price we are protecting ourselves from pressure or criticism. It's like being paid less is to expect less. And then, that's it. We feel shielded. They'll discover the imposter! At least I'll be an imposter on sale!

How many times in my life have I poorly negotiated a fee because I thought I was asking for too much? I thought they were "doing me a favor" by hiring me. Me, huh? Having to go there and beg? No way!

One time I got a call from the company I worked for saying they wanted to double my salary. That's right. A guy from HR called to say I would get a raise. At the time, I was very startled.

"Will I have to change positions or something like that?"

"No, it's just a raise."

"Wow... Of course, I accept but I was satisfied with my previous salary. Look, you can tell the bosses I never complained, okay?"

"It's just a salary equalization, Rafaella, so you will earn the same amount as other people who perform the same role as you."

Oops... I was, for a long time, earning LESS than everyone else! But I'd never question that. After all, they had already given me this great opportunity to work for them. I wouldn't be ungrateful.

As time went by and, of course, as my self-perception increased, I realized my HIGH-VALUE and stopped being afraid of charging a HIGH VALUE (genius and punny, huh?).

At the beginning, I'd still send the budget and put at the end: amount open to negotiation.

Today, I just send it. Of course, I am often asked to negotiate. It is a common practice in the market. But it is also common to receive a simple message:

"Done, Rafa!"

Next you will find some tips on how and how much to charge.

Be professional

You may be just starting out, no problem. But always have a business card and, if possible, a professional email (it makes a much better impression than @hotmail, @gmail, @etc.com). Invest a little in order to stand out.

If you don't want to, don't give your price in the moment

I've already made a lot of mistakes with this. The person asks how much it is and we feel obligated to answer right away. Being there, face to face. For an imposter, this is even more nerve-racking. There's no problem responding later. We need to sit down and do the math. In fact I prefer to say: "I'll send you the budget today". And I always send a nice little message of someone appreciating my work alongside the quote. You can, for example, say how much experience you have or attach photos of recent work. Something that shows that you understand the subject and are successful.

If needed, delegate this role to someone else

"Rafa, I really don't know how to charge. I'm terrified of it."
Ask someone for help. A friend, a relative or, if possible, an employee who can negotiate. A secret: you can use an email with just the company name, without your personal signature. At the end, you can just write "Thank you" and add the company's signature. This disconnects you from the proposal, and shows the customer that they are dealing with the company. This has already helped me a lot!

Know your worth

I have a degree in Administration and, even so, I have failed to calculate my costs in a correct and healthy way, leaving out things like transportation, equipment, food, etc. You need to take into consideration EVERYTHING you need to carry out the job and then state your price. If you work from home, be sure to include the costs of using your space.

"But, Rafa, I don't pay anything!"

Oh really? Who pays the electricity, water and internet bills?

If the workload goes up, raise the price

Who has never closed on a job that, at first, was something super simple, very quick, and ended up taking much more time than initially established?

Don't be embarrassed. The ideal is to have a pre-established value for each extra activity. For example: an hour of therapy costs X. If at the end of the session the patient asks you to "just take a look" at something, and that takes another ten minutes, offer them a longer session and, of course, charge extra for it.

Don't explain yourself

Pass along your price without explaining yourself. Instead of doing that, praise your work, its quality and its value. It is very common to see a professional with the impression that she is offending the client by giving the price. A manicurist, for example, explains herself by saying: "It's R$50. You know, there's the cost of the nail polish, which is expensive, and there's also the transportation to get here, etc.". Instead, she could have just said, "You'll love it. After having their nails done with me for the first time my clients don't let go. The cost is R$50." Period.

EMBRACE YOUR BLUNDERS

In 2015, the British newspaper Sunday Times carried out a survey with 3,000 people to find out what their biggest fear was. 41% responded that it was public speaking. Do you have any idea what this means?

People are more afraid of speaking in public than of dying.

In fact, the fear of public speaking is the fear of judgment, fear of ridicule, fear of making mistakes. But have you ever noticed how much fun we have when someone messes up? Often, this happens because we relate to the scene. When a person is the center of attention, we tend to think that they are special, they are better than us. If they make a mistake, it can bring us closer together. It's no wonder we love seeing bloopers of our favorite TV shows, right?

So, use errors to your advantage! Use it to connect with people. If you are in an important moment and make a mistake, just say: "Woah! I just got sidetracked. That's not it". Make the correction and move on.

Do you know why this strategy is worth it? People feel a huge connection to vulnerability. We feel comfortable seeing that the person in the spotlight is also vulnerable. It's not like you're going to plan for a mistake, but if it happens, don't freak out. Take advantage of the moment to captivate your audience. And, if the strategy doesn't work, at least not with everyone, know that it's someone else's problem and don't take it personally. Anyone who doesn't sympathize with vulnerability isn't worth it. The important thing is that you do not see it as your flaw, but as someone else's difficulty in having empathy.

Often, when I don't have all the necessary information to talk about a subject, I bring up my life. I share personal experiences. Everyone has a good story to tell. Even if you haven't studied or prepared, everything you've experienced so far gives you enough baggage to speak.

Another tip: before you start speaking, take a deep breath and control your breathing. This is an ancient technique for reducing anxiety. In fact, it can be used for all situations in your life, as you can never breathe too much. Close your eyes and remember the gratification you once felt when you did something well! Allow this moment to spread throughout your body.

Finally, declare your fear! Insecurity often makes things difficult, and we are not always able to eliminate it before speaking. To get around this, when starting a speech or presentation, if you are afraid of speaking in public, the best thing to do is to admit it. It's not saying you're afraid, but freeing yourself from inner pressure. This is yet another strategy to activate connection through vulnerability.

At the end of the day, what is a blunder? If it's stumbling a little on the path towards my dreams, then I'll never avoid it. On the contrary, I will happily blunder. As long as I blunder, I'll know I'm on the right path.

DO YOU PREFER 0 OR 50?

Have you ever heard of procrastination?

It's the habit of putting off for later, for tomorrow, for next week, for never again what could be done now. It's the old "dragging your feet".

It seems like it's just another bad habit for our collection (which one day, who knows, maybe I'll solve). But it's a serious problem. They say that 20% of the world's population admits to procrastinating. I personally believe that the other 80% are just procrastinating their confession...

What do people procrastinate on? Virtually everything: personal commitments, professional tasks, exercising, reading a book, planting a tree, washing the dishes, taking care of your health, financial planning, calling relatives, apologizing, taking a course, setting up a website.

Procrastination seems to be something we are not ashamed of. It is not seen as offensive when we hear: "Look, what a procrastinator!" Maybe that's why we don't take it as seriously as we should. But what if I replaced it with "fear" or "selfishness"?

"LOOK AT THEM, WHAT A FEARFUL PERSON!"
"WOW, WHAT A SELFISH PERSON!"

Maybe your thinking will change.

Want to see an example of mine?

I used to think: *The moment I sit down to write my book, I'll be unstoppable!* My book was already a success in my mind. I mentally polished the literary awards accumulated on the shelves of my imagination.

The thing was...

I DIDN'T HAVE A STUPID BOOK!
(Sorry sweet book, mommy loves you!)

Seriously, what was stopping me from sitting down and implementing all this success I was imagining?

It could only be the thing that I have mentioned thousands of times here: fear.

Fear of failure, fear of not being that successful, fear of having more work than I imagined, fear of realizing that I didn't have that much content to fill a book... Ultimately the fear that every imposter carries within themselves.

So, in order to avoid dealing with the fear and continue with the nice feeling that I call "imaginary success", what did I do? I procrastinated. I put off writing the book so I didn't have to face reality, which is very different from the beautiful field of illusion.

Procrastination "protected" me from the fear of failure.

But I realized that, take note: until I tried, I had already failed!

In our minds, things will work out 100% right (when we actually sit down and do it, of course). But in real life, we only have half the chance: 50% of it going right and 50% of it going wrong.

What do you prefer? The 100% of the illusion (which is equivalent to 0% in the real world) or the 50% that can work?

If you're down for the 50%, come with me.

1. Plan small rewards

We generally push aside things that are complicated and that will only pay off later (like filing our income tax, which will only be refunded in the second half of the year), to gratify ourselves with things that give us an immediate return. Watch a funny video. Eat some chocolate. Buy colored pens (that's me). And then you continue to procrastinate the important things with thousands of little things that will bring instant gratification.

Reverse the game. Create small rewards that will bring you closer to completing the larger task. Like: with each chapter I complete of my book, I'm going to buy a new pen (that's why I'm sitting here with 30 new pens).

In other words: instead of celebrating only when the final task is completed, set small goals and celebrate when you achieve each one.

2. Search for inevitability

It's even easier to procrastinate when we're not held accountable to anyone. Seeking inevitability is finding things that leave us with no way out. For example: I can avoid declaring income tax for two months. But there is a deadline there, and if I don't submit the declaration by that day, I could be investigated, fined, arrested, etc.

Do this with your dream. Commit to someone, post on social media what you are going to do. Create strategies that make it impossible to postpone things any longer. I, for example, posted: "Guys, my book will come out in September!" And now? Now, Rafa, get your butt to that computer, because you have a book to publish in September.

Do you want to make it more difficult?

Put your money on the line. That's right: BET. Take your favorite dress, give it to your sister and say: "If I don't make X by this day, you can't give me this dress back."

3. Count to 5

Actually, it's a countdown: start at 5 and count to 1.

5

4

3

2

1

LET'S GO DO THIS!

And that's how you have this book in your hands today!

MIRROR, MIRROR...

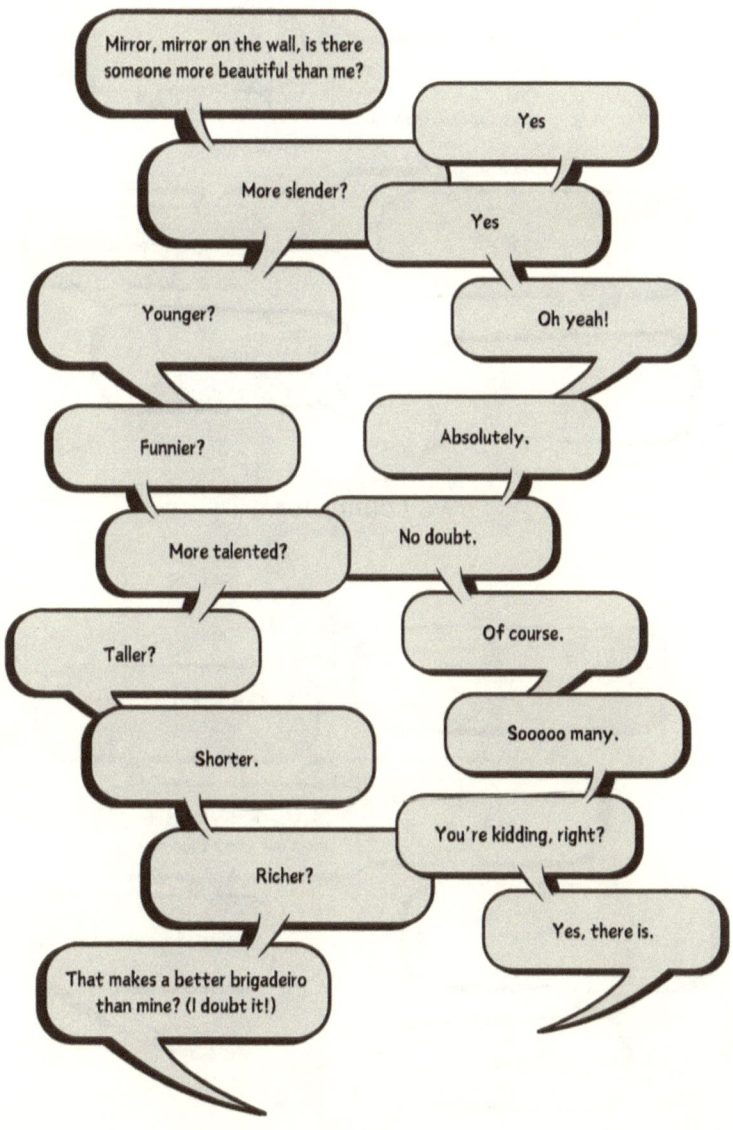

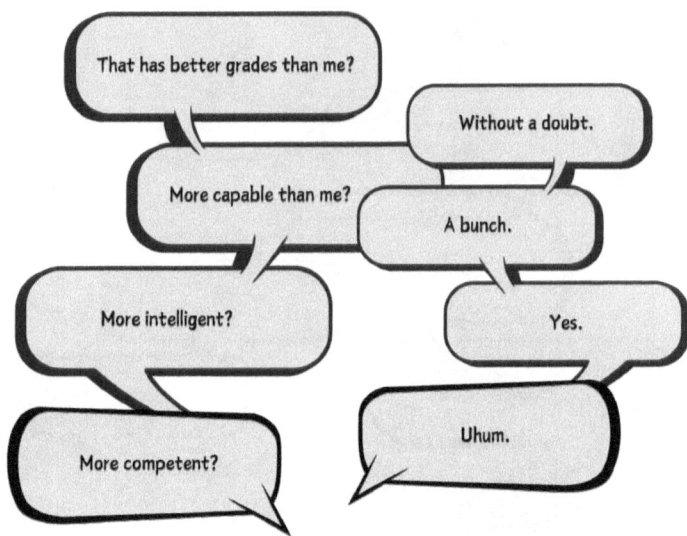

Two hours later…

Four hours later…

THE APPEARANCE CRUTCH

I was once preparing to host a show on live TV. There was everything you can imagine. Makeup, costumes. Suddenly a dress arrived for me to wear. Now imagine a beautiful dress! Simple. Not too flashy. Fits perfectly!

That day I loved the makeup that was done (I have a hard time liking makeup, I'm annoying about that). But that day it was perfect, very natural.

I looked in the mirror and thought I was beautiful. I was used to running on the street as a reporter. Zero glamour. But this was a prime-time show. A show about concerts! I felt like Beyoncé.

Some directors came into my dressing room. They leave. They come back and say:

"Rafa, we know you liked it. Truly, you look beautiful! But unfortunately, it's too beautiful."

"Huh?"

"That's right. Let's see if you can wear something simpler."

"But this dress is simple. There's no sparkles, there's no print."

"You make a good point. But we're going to have to change it. And we're going to ask them to redo your makeup."

"What?"

"Yeah, to make it more natural."

"But isn't it natural?"

"Yes, it's great. But it could be less..."

At the time, I was super upset. Come on! I couldn't understand how a person could say "You look beautiful, but change everything" without giving a plausible explanation.

Anyway, I must've smudged my makeup with my eyes full of tears. I felt super insecure.

But that night changed my life.

The penny finally dropped! I believe it was one of the biggest reasons that gave me the courage to write this book. I thought: *What do I have to offer this job?*

Beauty was not on my list of skills. If I were more put together or prettier, what would change for my audience?

Nothing!

What I needed was to be in high spirits! Happy! Excited! Spontaneous! That was what set me apart.

I turned to the costume designer (who, at this point, was feeling sorry for me):

"Bring over what they want. I don't care! We can change the makeup... F*ck it!"

It was one of the days where I gave my best. I simply let go. As if I'd felt that the things I had to say and the way I was going to say them were above my appearance. As if I were on the radio. I had to care about the content, not the look.

That's how I got rid of my appearance crutch.

I've heard many stories of women who didn't go to parties, didn't post their videos, didn't attend special events because they thought they were too fat, too thin, had grown out roots, had pimples on their faces... These external characteristics prevented them from shining with all of their vast internal potential.

FOLLOW YOUR CYCLE

It's beautiful how all things in nature have their own cycle.

The moon has its phases.

The sea has tides.

The year has seasons.

Yet, some women pretend they don't menstruate.

I've already shared that it's sad how menstruation is still a taboo topic. Like, everyone knows that many women menstruate, but we pretend they don't. You've most likely had to change your pad in the middle of the day at school. Or you had to ask a friend for one! My God, it looked like we were trafficking drugs!

Not to mention that we don't use the word "menstruation". It's like Lord Voldemort from *Harry Potter*, "he who must not be named." We refer to it using euphemisms, such as:

That time of the month

Shark week

Lady business (so official)

Monthly visitor (like, the mailman?)

On my period

Aunt Flow is visiting (tell her I said hi!)

Mother Nature

Crimson wave

Code red (everyone takes cover!)

Red tide

Having the painters in (huh?)

In Brazil, we also say "de chico" (I'm with chico), which stems from the Portuguese word "chiqueiro" (pigpen).

"Wow, Rafa, I never thought about it like that."

Exactly. It also took me years to wake up from all this denial. I recently participated in a campaign where we remembered that up until very recently advertisements for sanitary pads showed their products absorbing a blue liquid... *What the fuck?*

These and many other euphemisms on the topic keep us out of touch with nature, the cycle, and fertility. FERTILITY: this is the significance we should give to menstruation. It's almost the opposite of pregnancy. But while many want to caress a pregnant woman's belly, menstruation is *dirty* and needs to be hidden, interrupted, and concealed.

I'm not an extremist. I do not determine how each person should relate to their own body. You may love having your period or maybe not. You may hate it and you may even use techniques to avoid menstruating. It doesn't matter, as long as you don't make your choice because you feel diminished because of your flow.

At one point, I got fed up with having my period every month and had an intrauterine device inserted. I must've thought: *I hope I return as a man in the next incarnation.* Heavy, huh? However, over time, I questioned myself on the associations I made with menstruation, with my relationship with it, with being a woman. Ultimately, I fell in love with who I am.

I became so enthused with this hormonal variation that not only did I remove the device, but today I see this period of the month as a symbol of renewal. The only blood that does not come from violence, accidents, or disease, but from fertility and the possibility of new life.

With this feeling, I studied to better understand how female hormones work not only on the days of menstruation, but throughout the month. Based on this, I developed my monthly calendar.

I get astonished at how our "super modern" society never thought about this. Women live as if they were acyclical. But, for those who menstruate, IT MAKES A HUGE DIFFERENCE!

So, why not leverage the peculiarities of our cycle to our advantage?

It's possible! Come with me and I'll show you how.

A woman of three phases

Your menstrual cycle starts on the day you get your period. It then goes through a series of hormonal ups and downs, which are divided into three phases.

PREOVULATORY

This phase begins the day you get your period and continues until the day you start ovulating. It varies but often lasts approximately eleven days.

The first three days are the hardest. This is when we get bloated, feel cramps and other symptoms associated with menstruation. Our hormonal load – as well as our disposition – is low.

Between the 4th and 6th day, things start to improve. This is because your body begins to produce estrogen, which is a stimulating hormone. With it, your disposition grows, your reasoning ability improves and you begin to feel confident. Since your reasoning sharpens, this is a great time to plan projects and start more intellectual activities. You know that mentoring program you were looking to do? Now is the time to start!

PERIOVULATORY

This phase is marked by ovulation and, conse-quently, the fertile period. It lasts, on average, five days.

It all starts with the increase of your testosterone. It gives a general boost to your body and mind: you feel more confident, more attractive. Not only do you feel, but you actually look more beautiful: your skin is more even and even your hair finally looks the way you love it. These are the days that you'll receive a compliment and respond: "Thank you! I woke up like this!".

Testosterone also increases your chances of gaining muscle mass. If you want to do that HIIT workout for an extra sculpt, or lift heavier at the gym, take advantage of this phase!

And in addition to all this, testosterone increases li-bido. You might feel more flirtatious and irresistible.

At this stage, take the opportunity to do activities that require confidence: make big decisions, do interviews, and execute projects. On these days, your estrogen (which is a stimulant, remember!) will be at its peak. So you will feel very productive. If you have a very big project in mind, which will require a lot of energy and a sharp mind, organize yourself to focus on it during those days, and count on the extra help of your hormones.

These are also the best days to do appearance-related activities, like having a photo shoot or trying on clothes.

POSTOVULATORY

The last phase is marked by the production of progesterone, and lasts until the end of the cycle (approximately twelve days).

After estrogen and testosterone peak in the ovulatory period, they tend to drop, and another hormone comes into play: progesterone. It is the opposite of the other two: it makes you more introspective, sensitive (physically and emotionally) and slows down the brain. With it, we become more irritated, bloated, get headaches and sensitivity in the body, especially in the breasts (in other words, PMS everyone!). We are not as productive as before, and all that "charm" from phase 2 gives way to a certain aggressiveness. You may find yourself more impatient in very crowded or noisy places.

A good way to control the aggressiveness during this phase is to release energy by doing heavier physical activities, such as a boxing class or deep cleaning the house.

On the other hand, to reduce sensitivity and irritability, put more relaxing activities on your agenda, such as meditation, a massage, a relaxing bath, a walk at sunset... Choose the activity that you find most relaxing. And, of course, cross out the most stressful tasks from your agenda, intellectual projects that require concentration, long meetings, and major decision-making. Your brain isn't as sharp as it was last week. Therefore, this is not the time to choose between getting married and buying a bicycle...

And, speaking of marriage, avoid at all costs, for the love of God, discussing your relationship. Since the testosterone has gone down, your sex drive has also gone to space. This will make you more irritated.

Around the 24th day of your cycle, your hormone production drops sharply. Then the most intense phase of PMS begins. With the absence of hormones, you may experience breast pain, a spike in irritability and sensitivity (this is when we become the saddest and most tearful). My suggestion: keep a good supply of chocolate bars within reach.

The idea is for you to use this information to organize your agenda and future activities according to your cycle. You can enhance some activities by taking advantage of the stimulating boost in estrogen or the confidence generated by testosterone. You can dedicate yourself to more introspective tasks (such as writing a book) during the progesterone phase, in addition to staying away from stressful situations and major decision-making.

On the following page, you'll find a template you can use to build your calendar, where the text consultation was done alongside Dr. Vivian Stochero.

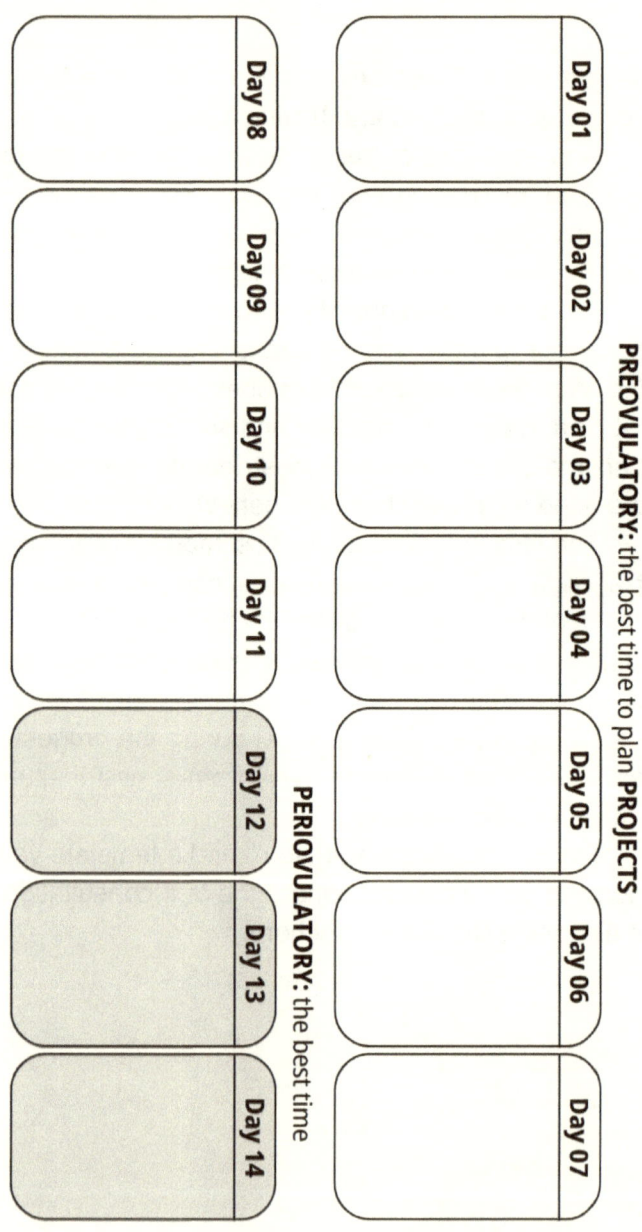

PREOVULATORY: the best time to plan **PROJECTS**

Day 01

Day 02

Day 03

Day 04

Day 05

Day 06

Day 07

Day 08

Day 09

Day 10

Day 11

PERIOVULATORY: the best time

Day 12

Day 13

Day 14

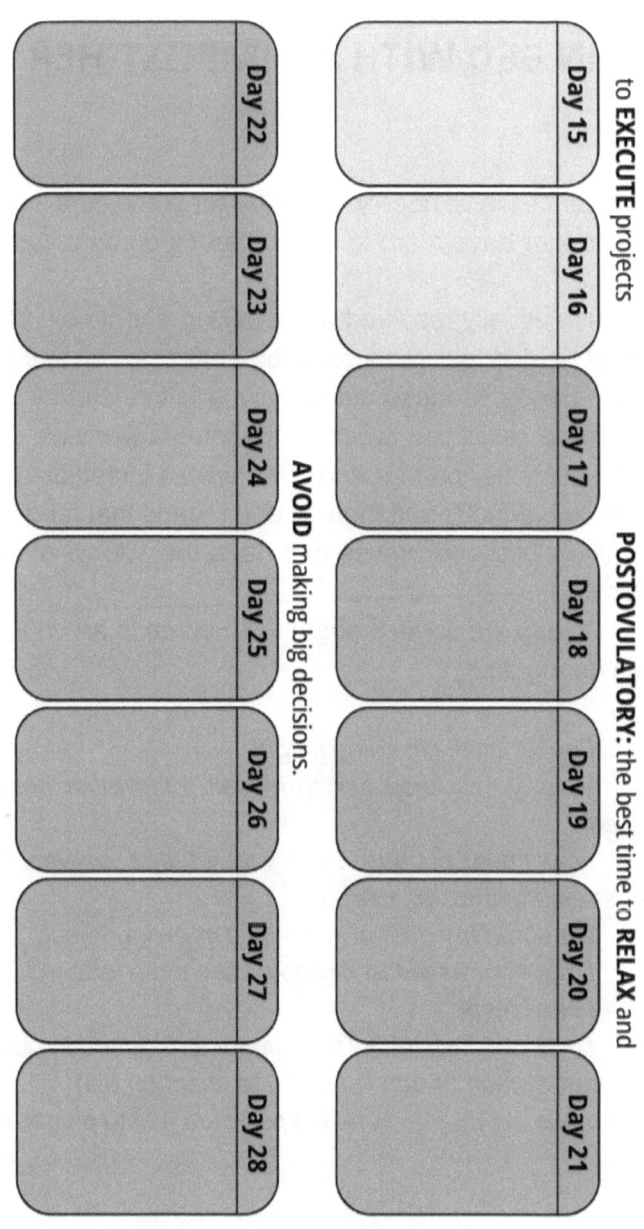

to **EXECUTE** projects

Day 15

Day 16

Day 17

Day 18

Day 19

Day 20

Day 21

POSTOVULATORY: the best time to **RELAX** and

Day 22

Day 23

Day 24

Day 25

Day 26

Day 27

Day 28

AVOID making big decisions.

IN BED WITH AN IMPOST-HER

Since we've been in the SSAI for some time, I believe we no longer have room to worry about judgment. Let's talk about it.

I'm usually reserved when talking about sex. But this moment behind four walls could be perfect for an imposter's "show". This is because our society is influenced by pornographic and sexist sex, which propagates a woman's obligation to satisfy her partner and offer him an incredible performance, full of faces and mouths and moans that feed the alpha male's ego and proves that he is the source of all this ecstasy.

These are some thoughts that come to an Imposter's minds during sex:

I never think I'm doing it right.

I worry and keep asking myself if the other person is satisfied.

I can't relax because I worry about my appearance (cellulite, stretch marks, fat, hair...).

I'm afraid my partner will think I'm exaggerating.

I'm embarrassed to say how I like to be touched.

I can't let go.

I'm afraid he'll think I'm naughty and determine that I'm not a good woman or that I'm going to cheat on him.

I feel like my partner is faking pleasure just to please me.

Then there is the most famous phrase, which inspired the subtitle on the cover of this book: *Why we never feel good enough?*

Most of the time, the problem is thinking too much about the other person, especially what they will think, instead of focusing on your own pleasure. This is made difficult by the fact that women are discouraged from exploring their own bodies.

Take ownership of your pleasure. Discover yourself. Touch yourself. Look for a gynecologist who can help you answer your questions without judgment and who respects your preferences and sexual orientation.

Pleasure is natural. It is within each of us. And even though, from time to time, it's fun to wear leather clothes, blindfolds and a whip, we don't need that disguise.

Blocks in experiencing pleasure do exist and can be a consequence of childhood trauma or past relationships. I do not aspire to address these types of matters in this book. However, I suggest that you look for a good professional to help you with this, if it's your situation to help you explore yourself better.

EVERY JUDGMENT IS A CONFESSION

If you've been to any of my lectures, classes or meetings, you know that this is the phrase I repeat the most. This is because, when I understood this phenomenon, I defeated most of the ghosts that haunted me.

I invite you to accompany me in this thought process. Reflect on it until you absorb everything. And please repeat this phrase to yourself as many times as needed.

Many of our obstacles, our knots, are due to this enormous fear of being judged. I like to give a very simple example: if you're walking down a deserted street and you trip and fall (a stupid little fall that doesn't even hurt), you'll probably get up, giggle a little and move on with your life.

Now this all changes if it's a crowded street, or if you trip and fall in the middle of the mall. You'll have the urge to dig a hole and disappear. This is because the laughter of others becomes bigger than the fall itself...

Another example is how maaaaany people are embarrassed to speak English when it's not their first language. They've studied a lot, but when it comes to speaking, they get stuck. My question to them is:

"Why do you get stuck?"

They usually make a thousand excuses, but you can be sure, they are afraid of judgement: "Are they going to laugh at me?", "I'm going to say everything wrong and embarrass myself".

Think about it: when we judge, we all go through a cognitive process that involves our culture, our life story, our context, our experiences, our values. It is impossible to make a judgment without involving who we are in it.

Here comes the big revelation: if every judgment unavoidably traces this internal path – TA-DA! –, it unveils all these different elements of the person who is judging. A person reveals a lot about themselves through the judgments they make.

When we start doing this exercise with our own judgements, prejudices and opinions, we are shocked! "My God, it really is impossible to separate judgment from myself!"

Then comes the relief: if someone laughs at you, and you're trying hard to learn a new language, or you just tripped and fell at the mall, let them solve their issues (lol). As for you, get out there and start speaking English or *hablando español.*

Stick it on your fridge, make a sticker for your car that says (I even have a t-shirt with this phrase):

Every judgement is a confession.

SCENES FROM THE MIND OF AN
~~IMPOSTER~~ **EX-IMPOSTER**
From the series "It's all part of my act"

Today is awards and bonuses day at the company. Let's see if I'm getting first or second place.

A thousand positive comments.. And ONE NEGATIVE! Man, I am a hit.

Uh, it's 9pm and I got an email from work. At this time? I'll respond tomorrow.

"Is your friend PMSing?"
"If she is or not, I don't know. But I'm certain you're an idiot!"

ADJUSTING THE THERMOMETER

Well, we've talked about trusting yourself and not comparing yourself to others.

We had a boost in our self-esteem.

"I AM INCREDIBLE! I'M WONDERFUL!"
"I DON'T CARE ABOUT JUDGMENT!"
"WOOHOO! I AM THE BEST!!!"

(HITS THE BRAKES)

HEY, PARTNER, CALM DOWN!
SIT DOWN. HAVE SOME WATER.
LET'S TALK.

The path to self-discovery – or, as I usually call it, your personal revolution – can be treacherous if we distort its real purpose. I have come across some people who are so "evolved" that they believe they are above others.

They suffer from Imposter Syndrome in reverse. I call it CONSULTANT Syndrome. They are so confident that they think they know more. They treat others with a tone of superiority.

Look at that trap. The great beauty of self-love and self-acceptance is knowing that we can evolve, that we are grateful for what we receive and achieve. But it's also knowing that there is always room to be an improved version of ourselves.

The best way to grow? Humility.

"Wait a minute, Rafa, you spent an entire book helping me learn to trust myself, to not care about other people's opinions, and now, in the final stretch, you're telling me to be humble? Do you want me to go back to thinking others are better than me?"

My dear ex-imposter, at this moment we understand that we are NOT worse than anyone, but I have to tell you: we are also NOT better than anyone.

"RAFA, I GIVE UP.

NOW THAT I'VE REALIZED I'M THE QUEEN OF THE WORLD?

THAT I'M SHE-RA?"

(OR SHIVA IF YOU'RE ZEN)

Come on down... I've felt this way, too. It's the famous rebound effect.

It doesn't help us at all. On the contrary, it makes us arrogant. Uncompromising. It prevents us from listening, learning, and evolving. Arrogance is the currency of the insecure. If you feel bad, you may try to create the illusion of being "better" because you need to

nurturing others to feel good.

True confidence is not thinking you are better than anyone else. It's knowing the difference between comparison and inspiration. Being the best version of yourself doesn't mean having to be better than others. Above all, know that everyone – including you – has a unique style. All styles have their place because they are all unique and can be eternally developed. And that's okay. In fact, that's where the true joy is. A confident person doesn't put anyone down, because they don't feel threatened by anyone.

The idea is that the more we love ourselves, the more we accept our vulnerabilities. When we don't know something, we don't blame ourselves, but we get excited about the idea of learning. We feel that we are on the same level as all human beings. With all of their glories and flaws.

Fighting imposter Syndrome doesn't mean believing you're better than someone else. It's considering yourself similar to everyone. If someone else can do it, I can too!

I'M WITH YOU

While writing this book, I traveled in my mind through many different faces, bodies, and personalities. I imagined so many women in different situations in my quest to get close to you! Maybe we don't even know each other, and this book came to you randomly, but if you saw yourself in anything you read, identified yourself, felt moved, in a way we are connected.

Somehow, I already feel like a part of your regaining confidence journey, I can picture you taking action. Shining. Loving yourself. I can see you looking in the mirror and winking, taking a deep breath before changing professions, and expressing your feelings. Knowing that you are worthy of affection, desire and admiration.

Believe me: you are in my prayers, meditations, texts, speeches. Every time I overcome my obstacles, I am also representing you, just as I feel represented by you.

Before we say goodbye, I wanted you to close your eyes for a few moments and visualize everything you dream of. Imagine yourself in places you never thought you would be, saying words you never imagined being able to say without disguises. Imagine being applauded, without any shame.

You can be sure, somewhere in this audience, I'll be applauding you.

NEW SHOW

The year was 2019. I was about to go on stage to present an award for Brazilian journalism. I peeked behind the curtain and saw, within seconds, the faces of almost every news anchor I grew up watching. Important people.

I thought:

"WHAT AM I DOING HERE?"

Why on earth did they invite me to present this? Was there a mix-up? Did the organizer look at my social media and see how simple my communication is and that I don't have a degree in Journalism?

Imagine how many mistakes I'm going to make! How much they will laugh at me later!

RAFA BRITES, YOU ARE A... YOU ARE A...

A woman who carries all the pressure of a historically sexist society.

You are neither better nor worse than anyone else. You are unique. That's why you're here today.

No one expects anything other than who you are, yourself, with your qualities and your flaws.

If someone judges you, be supportive of this confession. If you make a mistake, use it to your advantage by demonstrating vulnerability.

145

The best way to not fear your Imposter mask falling off is to go in right now, this instant, WITHOUT IT.

Be authentic.

Be integral!

Imposter Syndrome: I've welcomed and dominated you. Now, I won't be ashamed to shine.

The curtains open.

A feeling of freedom, generosity, and compassion came over me.

"Good evening, ladies and gentlemen. I am Rafa Brites."

HOW ABOUT YOU, READER?

WHO ARE YOU?

ABOUT THE AUTHOR

Rafa Brites was born in Porto Alegre, in the south of Brazil. She is a successful TV host and influencer. Over the course of her career, she has worked as a reporter for a morning show, and served as one of the co-hosts of several reality shows for two major Brazilian TV channels.

With a social media presence of over 2.3 million Instagram followers, her first book published in Brazil is already a best-seller. Now, she is furthering the message of women's empowerment to overcome the imposter syndrome with the English edition of her book titled *Impost-her Syndrome: Why We Never Feel Good Enough?*